THE ZEN OF BOOKKEEPING AND ACCOUNTING

BASIC ACCOUNTING FOR PRE-COLLEGE

AND NEW LEARNERS

Denver G. Pettigrew, Ph.D., CPA, MBA

I0511059

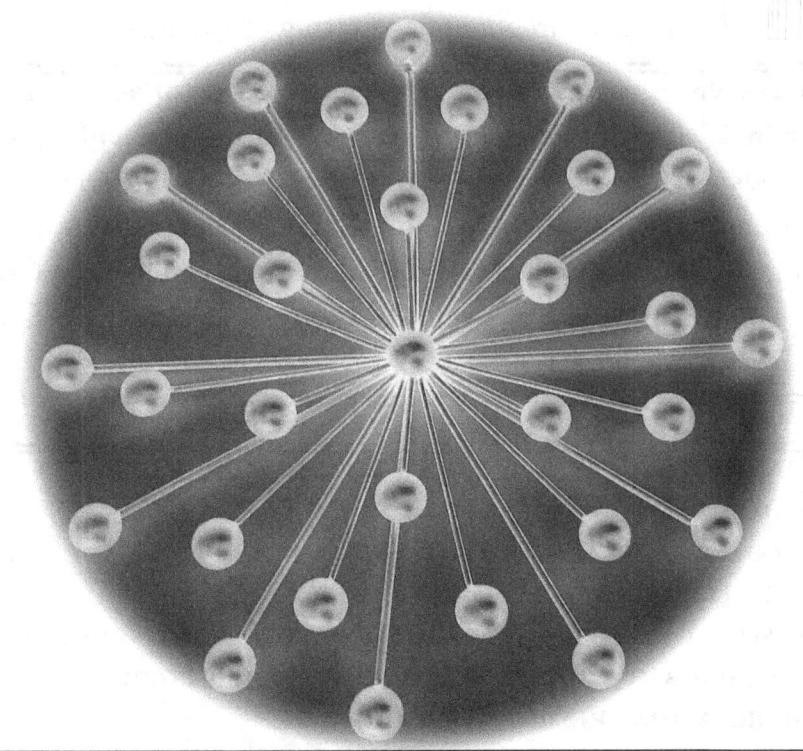

Collaborative learning: "Superior learners seek at least two to six additional sources of information." Dr. Denver Pettigrew

Denver Pettigrew, Ph.D., C.P.A., M.B.A.

THE ZEN OF BOOKKEEPING AND ACCOUNTING

BASIC ACCOUNTING FOR PRE-COLLEGE AND NEW LEARNERS
Denver G. Pettigrew, Ph.D., CPA, MBA

A life-long learner of business and economics-related topics, Dr. Pettigrew is a Certified Public Accountant (CPA); Doctor of Philosophy (Ph.D.) in Business Administration with a specialty in Advanced Accounting; Master's in Business Administration (MBA); and Bachelor of Science (BS) in Accounting. With over 25 years of working experience in accounting and over seven years as a successful professor of accounting and business at online and on-campus universities and colleges in the USA, Dr. Pettigrew hopes to motivate more students to consider careers in accounting or finance.

Accountants and bookkeepers use a systematic step-by-step set of activities to *record*, update, and report on the financial activities of an organization, maintained and reported in three main sets of financial records: (1) *Journals*, to *record* financial/economic transactions; (2) *General Ledger accounts*, to *post* the journal entries to the appropriate accounts; and (3) *Financial statements* including the balance sheet, income statement, statement of retained earnings, statement of changes in owners' equity account, and statement of cash flows to summarize and report on the activities in the general ledger.

- _BASIC_ SKILLS IN ARITHMETIC OR MATHEMATICS ARE REQUIRED TO LEARN BASIC BOOKKEEPING AND ACCOUNTING.
- AN EASY STEP-BY-STEP GUIDE FILLED WITH SIMPLE EXAMPLES IDEAL FOR PRE-COLLEGE STUDENTS AND NEW LEARNERS.
- IF YOU CAN READ, WRITE, AND USE A SIMPLE CALCULATOR TO ADD, SUBTRACT, MULTIPLY, AND DIVIDE, YOU CAN LEARN BASIC BOOKKEEPING AND ACCOUNTING BY FOLLOWING THE SIMPLE ILLUSTRATED INFORMATION PRESENTED IN THIS BOOK.
- CAN BE USED AS A SUPPLEMENTAL RESOURCE TO INTRODUCTORY COLLEGE ACCOUNTING TEXTBOOKS.

The Zen of Bookkeeping and Accounting: Basic Accounting for Pre-College and New Learners

ISBN-13: 978-1548966416

ISBN-10: 154896641X

Contents of The Zen of Bookkeeping and Accounting

Introduction to the Zen of Bookkeeping and Accounting

This book is designed mainly for pre-college and other learners and individuals who believe that accounting would be too difficult, if not impossible, for them to learn. This belief is often based on misperceptions of what bookkeeping and accounting is about and the levels and types of education needed to learn accounting. Reasons given by students for not studying accounting include:

- "I cannot learn accounting because I am not good at mathematics!"
- "Accounting is too hard to learn because it appears to be extremely complicated!"
- "I could never understand, learn, and remember all those technical words used in accounting!"

The information and presentations in the book will show that if you can read, write, and use a simple calculator to add, subtract, multiply, and divide, you can learn basic bookkeeping and accounting by following the information presented in this book. Simple words are used throughout the book to explain the accounting concepts and activities. Words like *you, I,* and *we* are occasionally used to identify the learner, author, and group in the activities in the chapters. This book also can be used a great supplemental resource to introductory college accounting textbooks.

The material in the book is based on a simple framework for teaching and learning accounting and bookkeeping using activities related to the elements of a *Simple Combined Chart of Accounting and Trial Balance* shown on the following page and throughout the book. Beginners tend to get overwhelmed at the number of concepts and theories contained in the chapters in accounting textbooks, that they lose sight of the *main reasons* for studying each chapter. I hope that by including "What is the purpose of this chapter?" in the first few lines of each chapter, the reader will see its purpose.

Accountants and bookkeepers use a systematic step-by-step set of activities to *record*, update, and report on the financial activities of an organization, maintained in three main sets of financial records: (1) *Journals* (JEs), to initially *record* financial or economic business transactions; (2) *General Ledger accounts* (GL), to *post* the journal entries to the appropriate accounts; and (3) *Financial statements* including the balance sheet, income statement, statement of retained earnings, statement of changes in the owners' equity account, and statement of cash flows, to summarize the GL accounts and report on the operations and financial health of the organization. The terms *firm, company,* and *organization* will be used interchangeably throughout the book.

The material is presented in a simple, straightforward manner and supported by many figures and examples. As the famous far-eastern saying goes "a picture is worth ten thousand words," I have used many examples and figures to demonstrate simple bookkeeping and accounting concepts and practices throughout the book and provide examples of the application of accounting and bookkeeping in the real world (Barnard, 1927).

I hope you enjoy reading the book and realize that you too can learn bookkeeping and accounting.

Best wishes for a successful career,

Dr. Pettigrew

Reference:

Barnard, F. R. (1927). One Picture is Worth Ten Thousand Words. *Printers Ink*, *10*, 114-115.

A simple Combined Chart of Accounts and Trial Balance

CHART OF ACCOUNTS	TRIAL BALANCE	
Account #, Classification and General Ledger Descriptions	Debit $$	Credit $$
Balance Sheet		
Assets: 1000		
• 1010 Cash	XXXX.XX	
• 1020 Accounts Receivable	XXXX.XX	
• 1021 Allowance for Bad Debts		XXXX.XX
• 1030 Merchandise Inventory	XXXX.XX	
• 1040 Prepaid Accounts	XXXX.XX	
• 1050 Fixed Assets	XXXX.XX	
• 1051 Accumulated Depreciation		XXXX.XX
Liabilities: 2000		
• 2010 Accounts Payable		XXXX.XX
• 2020 Salaries & Wages Payable		XXXX.XX
• 2030 Long-term Payable		XXXX.XX
• 2040 Unearned Revenue		XXXX.XX
Equity: 3000		
• 3010 Owner's Capital/Equity		XXXX.XX
• 3020 Drawing	XXXX.XX	
• 3030 Retained Earnings		XXXX.XX
Income Statement		
Revenue: 4000		
• 4010 Sales Revenue		XXXX.XX
• 4020 Other Revenue		XXXX.XX
• 4030 Cost of Goods Sold (COGS)	XXXX.XX	
Expenses: 5000		
• 5010 Rent Expense	XXXX.XX	
• 5020 Salaries & Wages	XXXX.XX	
• 5030 Office Expenses & Supplies	XXXX.XX	
• 5040 Telephone Expense	XXXX.XX	
• 5050 Insurance Expense	XXXX.XX	
• 5060 Advertising & Promotion Expense	XXXX.XX	
• 5070 Depreciation Expense	XXXX.XX	
• 5080 Vehicle, Travelling & Entertainment Expense	XXXX.XX	
• 5090 Bad Debt Expense	XXXX.XX	
	XXXX.XX	XXXX.XX

BALANCE SHEET

INCOME STATEMENT

Chapter 1: Fundamentals of Bookkeeping and Accounting

OK, Where Do I Start? A simple Example

Question: What is the purpose of this chapter?

Answer: To introduce you to the objectives of an accounting and bookkeeping system and important fundamental concepts and tools.

Before we can start recording the financial activities of the firm, we must define what accounting and bookkeeping is about. Because accounting and bookkeeping activities are inter-related and sometimes used synonymously, for simplification of explanations we will use the terms interchangeably although technically they are different. Accountants must know bookkeeping and attain a much higher level, and variety, of education and certification, to provide operating and strategic expertise to different levels of managers in firms.

The public uses the generic term *accounting* in business and non-business formats such as when we have to (a) *account* for our whereabouts last Wednesday, (b) *account* for how we did in the test on a particular date or particular subject, (c) *account* for what we did with the book we borrowed from the library last month, (d) *account* for how we spent the money that was in our bank account at the beginning of the month, (e) *account* for where we got the money to put into our bank accounts (sources) how we spent (uses) the money and how much is the remaining amount (balance) at the end of the month, etc. You get the idea that accounting for something is explaining the results of specific activities or money. In this book, we focus only on financial accounting: Accounting for the sources and uses of valuable monetary resources (values shown in dollars) in a business.

There are three fundamental concepts new learners *must* understand in learning accounting and bookkeeping: (1) business transactions, (2) the *double entry* concept of *debits* and *credits*, and (3) the *accounting equation*.

1. **Business Transactions** Bookkeepers record only transactions completed on behalf of a business firm—business transactions; not the personal transactions of the business owner.

2. **Double-entry System of Accounting** Business transactions consist of debits and equal amounts of credits. In other words, every transaction has an equal movement of value *to* (debit or DR) a receiving general ledger (GL) account *from* (credit or CR) a source GL account, to properly record the transaction in journal entries (JE); if we subtract all the credit entries from all the debit entries in a journal, the result must be

zero if recorded correctly. The journal entries are posted periodically to the corresponding general ledger accounts (GL) indicated in the journal.

DEBIT DR　　　　　　　　　　　　　　　　**CREDIT CR**

3. **The Accounting Equation** The accounting equation is based on the same double-entry system of accounting used for recording transactions in the journal and provides a summary of all amounts posted in GL accounts in a simple formula: Total Assets (A) equal the Total of Liabilities (L) plus Owners' Equity (E), or A = L + E.

> **Important**: You ***must*** fully understand how to make a simple journal using the double-entry concept of debit and credit.

The following is a simple demonstration of steps taken to record a few ordinary business transactions in a general journal. I will use a fictitious firm, MZ LLC., owned and operated by a fictitious person, Master Zen. New firms generally begin operations using cash for all transactions until the business is operating successfully. We will discuss this further in a later chapter, but for now, MZ LLC operates on a cash basis.

- On January 1, 20xx, Master Zen invests $20,000.00 of his savings into starting a firm, registered as MZ LLC., in Florida, to buy and sell books. He opens a bank account in the name of the firm and deposits the $20,000.00. He receives a checkbook and check register to keep track of receipts and payments for the firm. All receipts are promptly deposited to the account and all purchases and payments are done using the business checks
- On Jan. 2, 20xx MZ LLC buys 200 books for $2,000.00 using business check number 1. Note that whenever a business operates by buying and selling finished products, such as books, they are often referred to as merchandize and the firm is called a retailer of merchandize, or retailer, for short.
- On Jan. 5 MZ LLC sells 100 books for $3,000.00 cash and deposits the amount in the bank.

- On Jan. 7, the end of week 1, MZ LLC pays Mr. J. Bookkeeper $800.00 for services using business check number 2.

Let us first look at how these transactions are recorded in the check register supplied by the bank when the firm's account was opened. The transactions would be recorded as indicated in the *Check Register* shown below. We will create a simple general journal from information recorded in the check register using the chart of accounts shown on page 2 and Appendix A. Hint: Three key questions to consider when recording journals using the chart of accounts are (1) Which account is receiving cash or value? This account is *debited*. (2) Which account provided (source) the cash or value in (1)? This account is *credited*; and (3) What is the purpose of the transaction? This is explained on a separate line below the transactions.

A Typical Check Register

PLEASE MAKE SURE TO DEDUCT CHARGES THAT AFFECT YOUR ACCOUNT										
ITEM NO. OR TRANS. CODE (a)	DATE (b)	TRANSACTION DESCRIPTION (c)	ADDITIONS: AMT OF DEPOSITS OR INTEREST (+) (d)		✔ T	FEE IF ANY (-) (e)	SUBTRACTIONS: AMT OF PAYMENTS OR WITHDRAWALS (-) (f)		BALANCE (g)	
	Jan. 1, 20XX	Investment from Master Zen	20,000	00					20,000	00
Check # 1	Jan. 2	Books Unlimited- 200 books					2,000	00	18,000	00
	Jan. 5	Cash Sales 100 books	3,000	00					21,000	00
Check # 2	Jan. 7	Mr. J. Bookkeeper					800	00	20,200	00

The transactions in the check register would be recorded in a typical general journal using the GL account numbers shown in the chart of accounts (COA). Notice that *each* transaction involves the *cash* account either receiving cash or spending (paying) cash. Remember that each transaction must be recorded on a separate line and contains a debit *and* a credit. It is customary to record the debit entry first, followed by the corresponding credit entry and then the explanation for the entries. Carefully compare the check register with the following general journal.

General Journal

General Journal			Page No. 1		
Date 2017		Description	GL Ref.	Debit	Credit
Jan	1	Cash	1010	20,000.00	
		Owner's Capital	3010		20,000.00
		Cash Invested by Master Zen			

Jan	2	Merchandize Inventory	1030	2,000.00	
		Cash	1010		2,000.00
		Purchase books 200 from Books Unlimited			
Jan	5	Cash	1010	3,000.00	
		Sales Revenue	4010		3,000.00
		Cash sales of 100 books to customers			
Jan	7	Salaries & Wages Expense	5020	800.00	
		Cash	1010		800.00
		Salary paid to J. Bookkeeper			

Hint: Whenever a transaction narrative contains the words *cash* or *check*, or phrase such as *paid* to or *received money* from; one of the GL accounts in the transaction is the *cash account*! look at the following cash transaction examples to identify the accounts affected and position (DR or CR) when recording the related journal entries using the chart of accounts. We will use transaction numbers instead of dates for this practice exercise:

Cash Transactions

1. Paid check for $1,000.00 to landlord for a month's rent of office space.
2. Paid $75.00 for business telephone service to phone service provider.
3. Bought for cash $1,000.00 books to sell to customers.
4. Received $1,500.00 for sale of books to cash customers.
5. Paid $400.00 to local newspaper to advertise business to the public.
6. Paid electric bill for $200.00 to electric utility company.
7. Purchased a used van for cash, $3,000.00

Solutions using the chart of accounts

1. GL account *5010* is DR and GL account *1010* is CR for $1,000.00
2. GL account *5040* is DR and GL account *1010* is CR for $75.00
3. GL account *1030* is DR and GL account *1010* is CR for $1,000.00
4. GL account *1010* is DR and GL account *4010* is CR for $1,500.00
5. GL account *5060* is DR and GL account *1010* is CR for $400.00
6. GL account *5040* is DR and GL account *1010* is CR for $200.00
7. GL account *1050* is DR and GL account *1010* is CR for $3,000.00

Each transaction would be recorded on three separate lines: (a) debit entry, followed by (b) credit entry, then (c) explanation for the transaction.

You might be wondering, "What if the transactions were not paid for immediately in cash by the firm or by its customers?" Great question!

In that case, we would replace the cash account with a *non-cash* account from the balance sheet section of the chart of account as follows:

Non-Cash Transactions—On Terms (Payments Delayed)

1. ~~Paid check~~ Received bill for $1,000.00 to landlord for a month's rent of office space.
2. ~~Paid~~ Received bill for $75.00 for business telephone service to phone service provider.
3. Bought ~~for cash~~ on terms $1,000.00 books to sell to customers, firm will pay suppliers at a later date.
4. ~~Received~~ Sold $1,500.00 ~~for sale~~ of books on terms, amount ~~cash~~ to be received from customers at a future date.
5. ~~Paid~~ Received bill for $400.00 ~~to~~ from local newspaper to advertise business to the public.
6. ~~Paid~~ Received electric bill for $200.00 to electric utility company.
7. Purchased a used van for ~~cash~~ $3,000.00, firm to pay seller at a future date.

Solutions using the chart of accounts

1. GL account *5010* is DR and GL account ~~*1010*~~ *2010* is CR for $1,000.00
2. GL account *5040* is DR and GL account ~~*1010*~~ *2010* is CR for $75.00
3. GL account *1030* is DR and GL account ~~*1010*~~ *2010* is CR for $1,000.00
4. GL account ~~*1010*~~ *1020* is DR and GL account *4010* is CR for $1,500.00
5. GL account *5060* is DR and GL account ~~*1010*~~ *2010* is CR for $400.00
6. GL account *5040* is DR and GL account ~~*1010*~~ *2010* is CR for $200.00
7. GL account *1050* is DR and GL account ~~*1010*~~ *2010* is CR for $3,000.00

Each transaction would be recorded on three separate lines: (a) Debit entry, followed by (b) Credit entry, then (c) Explanation for the transaction.

Notice that for non-cash transactions, the *Cash* account *1010* is replaced by the *Accounts Receivable* GL account *1020* for the delayed *receipt* of cash from customer, and the GL *Accounts Payable* account *2010* replaces the Cash account *1010* for the delayed *payments*.

We will describe Accounts Receivable and Accounts Payable in more detail in Chapter 4.

3 Key Questions when Recording Journals

> Three key questions to consider when recording journals using the chart of accounts are (1) Which account is receiving cash or value? This account is debited. (2) Which account (source) provided the cash or value in (1)? This account is credited; and (3) What is the purpose of the transaction? This is explained in a separate line below the transactions.

> Accountants and bookkeepers use a systematic step-by-step set of activities to *record*, update, and report on the financial activities of an organization, maintained in three main sets of financial records: (1) *Journals,* to *record* financial/economic transactions; (2) *General Ledger accounts,* to *post* the journal entries to the appropriate accounts; and (3) *Financial statements* comprising the balance sheet, income statement, statement of retained earnings, and statement of cash flows to summarize and report on the balances in the general ledger.

The definition used for this simplified book is in terms of the activities involved in the accounting *process*: Accounting is both a process and a means of summarizing and reporting of financial transactions and activities of a business for a specific period. The process involves identifying and recording financial transactions in *journals* and posting them to related accounting *ledgers*; the accounting ledgers are then summarized, classified, and reported in financial statements such as the *balance sheet, income statement, statement of changes in owner's equity*, and *cash flows statement* to be used by users for decision-making purposes. In other words, accounting is a systematic step-by-step set of activities by the accountant to (1) identify, analyze, and record financial transactions, (2) record the transactions in the journal using a chart of accounts, (3) post the journal entries to the general ledger, (4) prepare a trial balance of the general ledger accounts, (5) make adjustments at the end of accounting periods, and (6) summarize and report on the activities of the firm using financial statements.

Notice that the process begins with identifying and recording financial transactions of the business.

Steps in the accounting process can be illustrated as follows:

Steps in The Accounting Process					
STEP 1	STEP 2	STEP 3	STEP 4	STEP 5	STEP 6
Analyze Transactions	Record Journal Entries	Post to General Ledger	Prepare Trial Balance	End-of Period Adj. Entries	Compile Financial Statements

---

The general ledger accounts shown in the combined chart of accounts and trial balance are sometimes referred to as *elements* in the balance sheet and income statement. The Cash account, Accounts Receivable, Merchandise Inventory, Accounts Payable, Long-term Payable etc. are referred to as *elements* in the balance sheet. Likewise, Sales Revenue, Cost of Goods Sold, Rent Expense, Salaries and Wages etc. are referred to as *elements* in the income statement.

To correctly analyze, record, and post transactions of a firm, new learners must know and fully understand what I believe to be are the two most important concepts in accounting: (1) the *double-entry system of accounting,* and (2) the *accounting equation.* These two concepts are fundamental and directly related and must be fully understood and memorized to successfully learn accounting.

The Double-entry Concept of Accounting

The double-entry concept states that every business transaction involves an *equal* exchange of value between the two sides of every transaction: a receiver and a giver. Business transactions are therefore referred to as give-get activities because when value is given, the same value must be received by someone on the other side of the transaction. In accounting, the give-get transactions are recorded in the journal and posted in representing general ledger accounts. The account *receiving* the value is *debited* and the account *giving* the value is *credited* for an equal amount. Accountants look at the *chart of accounts* to identify the general ledger accounts in which to record *transactions*—debiting one or more accounts receiving value and simultaneously crediting one or more accounts giving up the value.

THE DOUBLE-ENTRY SYSTEM OF ACCOUNTING: DEBITS MUST EQUAL CREDITS		
DEBIT DR	⬅	***CREDIT CR***
DEBITS (LEFT)	MUST EQUAL (BALANCE)	CREDITS (RIGHT)
GET	MUST EQUAL (BALANCE)	GIVE
RECEIVE	MUST EQUAL (BALANCE)	SOURCE
IN	MUST EQUAL (BALANCE)	OUT
TO	MUST EQUAL (BALANCE)	FROM

A "T" account structure (because it looks like a giant T) is generally used to provide a visual representation of the general ledger accounts to assist students in understanding the recording process using debits (DR) and credits (CR). In the T format it is easier for the student to see the Debits on the left side of the ledger account and the Credits on the right side;

sometimes, the sides might be labeled DR and CR. To remember which side is debited or credited, the words *credit* and *right* both contain the letter "R".

Two popular styles of the conceptual "T" general ledger accounts are: the horizontal and vertical or perpetual "T" (in **bold**) styles are shown in the following diagrams.

Example of The Horizontal or Balancing "T" Style of General Ledger Account								
Account Name: Fixed Assets					Account No.: 1050			
Date 2017		Trans. Description	JL Ref.	*Debit*	Date 2017		Trans. Description	JL Ref.	*Credit*
Jan.	1	General Journal	J1	2,000.00	Jan.	1			

Example of The Vertical or Perpetual General Ledger Account "T" Style							
Account Name: Fixed Assets					Account No.: 1050		
				Post JL here		Updated Balance	
Date 2017		Trans. Description	JL Ref.	*Debit*	*Credit*	*Debit*	*Credit*
Jan.	1	General Journal	J1	2,000.00		2,000.00	

Notice with the vertical or perpetual style of general ledger accounts, also referred to as *four* columns style because it has two sets of debit and credit columns, the updated balance columns on the right side of the account contains the *updated* or *running* (also called *perpetual*) balance in the account *after* the posting of the journal transaction to the general ledger account.

The Accounting Equation

The accounting equation concept, *Assets = Liabilities (debts) + Owners' Equity*, demonstrates the relationship between groups of items and their values owned by the firm for use in the business—assets, and the sources of financing for the assets—liabilities plus owners' equity. Ledger accounts for assets usually have debit balances, and the ledger accounts for liabilities (debts) and owners' equity (capital) normally have credit balances. It is called an *equation* because, if you recall the double-entry system of accounting concept discussed in the previous section, the total of the accounts with debit balances must equal the total of the accounts with credit balances.

The Accounting Equation				
ASSETS	=	LIABILITIES	+	EQUITY
LIABILITIES	=	ASSETS	-	EQUITY
EQUITY	=	ASSETS	-	LIABILITIES

The accounting equation can be viewed as a summary of a firm's balance sheet on a specific date. For instance, if a firm owns fixed assets valued at $100,000.00 (office building $60,000.00, automobile $40,000.00), the sources of the funding for these assets might have been from cash down-payment from the owners (equity) of $10,000.00 toward purchase of the office building and a mortgage loan from the bank for $50,000.00 (liability), for a total purchase price of $60,000.00 ($10,000.00 + $50,000.00) for office building; cash down-payment from the business owners (equity) on the automobile of $5,000.00 with financing from the car dealer of $35,000.00 (liability) for the total purchase price of $40,000.00 ($5,000.00 + $35,000.00) for the automobile.

The accounting equation would show: **Assets $100,000.00** (building $60,000 + automobile $40,000) = **Liabilities $85,000.00** (mortgage $50,000 + $35,000.00 automobile financing $35,000.00) + **Owners' Equity $15,000.00** (cash down-payment for office building $10,000 + cash down-payment automobile $5,000.00).

Summary Overview of Accounting Activities

Accountants use **Charts of Accounts** when analyzing business transactions to determine which accounts to record them in the general journal and post periodically to the general ledger accounts listed in the chart of accounts. At the end of an accounting period the balances in each general ledger account are listed on a report called a trial balance (TB) and used to determine that the total of all accounts with debit balances equals the total of all accounts with credit balances.

Adjusting entries are also made at the end of the accounting period to a few general ledger (GL) balances to ensure that revenues and expenses and the related assets and liabilities are correctly posted (matched) to the appropriate accounting periods (current or future), and an *adjusted trial balance* created that lists all GL balances *after* the adjustments.

The general ledger accounts for revenues and expenses listed on the adjusted trial balance are then summarized on the *income statement* (IS) to determine the *net income* (or loss) for the period, which is then added to (or subtracted from) the balance for the retained earnings, a balance sheet (BS) account.

The final adjusted retained earnings account balance, along with the other balance sheet (BS) accounts on the adjusted TB, are summarized on the *balance sheet* statement to report the status of the assets, liabilities, and owner's equity on a specific date of the financial period.

Summary questions of financial activities chapter 1

1) How much cash (value) did the owner invest (capital) to start the business?

   a) Which accounts contain this value?

2) What are the three main sections of the balance sheet?

   a) _____

   b) _____

   c) _____

Practice Journalizing Transactions 1

Reminder of steps: Each transaction would be recorded on three separate lines: (a) Debit entry, followed by (b) Credit entry, then (c) Explanation for the transaction.

1. Paid check for $1,000.00 to landlord for a month's rent of office space.
2. Paid $75.00 for business telephone service to phone service provider.
3. Bought for cash $1,000.00 books to sell to customers.
4. Received $1,500.00 for sale of books to cash customers.
5. Paid $400.00 to local newspaper to advertise business to the public.
6. Paid electric bill for $200.00 to electric utility company.
7. Purchased a used van for cash, $3,000.00

Practice Journalizing Transactions using the chart of accounts

1. GL account _____ is DR and GL account _____ is CR for $
2. GL account _____ is DR and GL account _____ is CR for $
3. GL account _____ is DR and GL account _____ is CR for $
4. GL account _____ is DR and GL account _____ is CR for $
5. GL account _____ is DR and GL account _____ is CR for $
6. GL account _____ is DR and GL account _____ is CR for $
7. GL account _____ is DR and GL account _____ is CR for $

Answers to Summary questions of financial activities chapter 1

1) How much cash (value) did the owner invest (capital) to start the business? $20,000.00

    a) Which accounts contain this value? Cash account #1010 debit $20,000.00 and Owners Capital account #3010 credit $20,000.00.

2) What are the three main sections of the balance sheet?

    a) Assets

    b) Liabilities

    c) Equity

Solutions to Practice Journalizing Transactions using the chart of accounts

1. GL account 5010 is DR and GL account 1010 is CR for $1,000.00
2. GL account 5040 is DR and GL account 1010 is CR for $75.00
3. GL account 1030 is DR and GL account 1010 is CR for $1,000.00
4. GL account 1010 is DR and GL account 4010 is CR for $1,500.00
5. GL account 5060 is DR and GL account 1010 is CR for $400.00
6. GL account 5040 is DR and GL account 1010 is CR for $200.00
7. GL account 1050 is DR and GL account 1010 is CR for $3,000.00

General Journal

		General Journal		Page No. 1			
Date 20xx		Description	GL Ref.	**Debit**		**Credit**	
				Amount		Amount	
	1	Rent Expense	5010	1,000	00		
		Cash	1010			1,000	00
		Paid Month's rental for office space					
	2	Utilities Expense	5040	75	00		
		Cash	1010			75	00
		Paid for telephone service					
	3	Merchandize Inventory	1030	1,000			
		Cash	1010			1,000	00
		Purchased books for cash					
	4	Cash	1010	1,500	00		
		Sales Revenue	4010			1,500	00
		Cash sales of Books					

	5	Advertising & Promotion Expense	5060	400	00		
		Cash	1010			400	00
		Paid for newspaper advertising					
	6	Utilities Expense	5040	200	00		
		Cash	1010			200	00
		Paid electricity bill for month					
	7	Fixed Asset	1050	3,000	00		
		Cash	1010			3,000	00
		Purchased used van for cash					

Summary

- Accountants use a systematic step-by-step set of activities taken by the accountant to (1) identify, analyze, and record financial transactions, (2) record the transactions in the journal using a chart of accounts, (3) post the journal entries to the general ledger, (4) prepare a trial balance, (5) record and post end-of-period adjusting and closing entries, and (6) summarize and report on the activities of the firm by compiling financial statements.

- The concepts of the *double-entry system of accounting* and the *accounting equation* are used to record, update, and report on the three main set of *books* used to account for the operations of an organization: (1) *Journal* to record transactions, (2) *General Ledger* to post the journal entries, and (3) *Financial statements* to summarize and report on the balances in the general ledger.

Cumulative Comprehensive Hands-on Example 1

Master Zen started a for-profit business firm, MZ LLC., in the state of Florida, January 1, 2017, with $20,000.00 cash as equity capital. The business used $2,000.00 to purchase office desks and chairs. Show the accounting equation for MZ LLC.

Solutions to Cumulative Hands-On Example 1

Assets $20,000.00 (cash $18,000.00 + office furniture $2,000.00) = Liabilities $0.00 + owners' equity $20,000.00. See effects on the combined COA and TB on the following page.

A Simple Combined Chart of Accounts and Trial Balance MZ LLC.

CHART OF ACCOUNTS	TRIAL BALANCE	
Account #, Classification, and General Ledger Descriptions	Debit $$	Credit $$
Balance Sheet		
Assets: 1000		
• 1010 Cash	18,000.00	
• 1020 Accounts Receivable	XXXX.XX	
• 1021 Allowance for Bad Debts		XXXX.XX
• 1030 Merchandise Inventory	XXXX.XX	
• 1040 Prepaid Accounts	XXXX.XX	
• 1050 Fixed Assets	2,000.00	
• 1051 Accumulated Depreciation		XXXX.XX
Liabilities: 2000		
• 2010 Accounts Payable		XXXX.XX
• 2020 Salaries & Wages Payable		XXXX.XX
• 2030 Long-term Payable		XXXX.XX
• 2040 Unearned Revenue		XXXX.XX
Equity: 3000		
• 3010 Owner's Capital/Equity		20,000.00
• 3020 Drawing	XXXX.XX	
• 3030 Retained Earnings		XXXX.XX
Income Statement		
Revenue: 4000		
• 4010 Sales Revenue		XXXX.XX
• 4020 Other Revenue		XXXX.XX
• 4030 Cost of Goods Sold (COGS)	XXXX.XX	
Expenses: 5000		
• 5010 Rent Expense	XXXX.XX	
• 5020 Salaries & Wages	XXXX.XX	
• 5030 Office Expenses & Supplies	XXXX.XX	
• 5040 Utilities Expense	XXXX.XX	
• 5050 Insurance Expense	XXXX.XX	
• 5060 Advertising & Promotion Expense	XXXX.XX	
• 5070 Depreciation Expense	XXXX.XX	
• 5080 Vehicle, Travelling & Entertainment Expense	XXXX.XX	
• 5090 Bad Debt Expense	XXXX.XX	
	$20,000.00	$20,000.00

Right margin labels: BALANCE SHEET, INCOME STATEMENT

Chapter 2: Business Transactions, Chart of Accounts, and General Journal

Business Transactions

Question: What is the purpose of this chapter?

Answer: To demonstrate how business transactions are recorded and posted in a typical accounting system.

Business transactions are activities performed on behalf of a firm that are measured or valued by money. Business transactions are expenditures (or expenses) or receipts for goods or services for cash, or contractual obligations to be paid or received at a later date—on terms. These business transactions are recorded by the accountant in the books of the business on journal entries guided by the chart of accounts. Business transactions are usually supported (evidenced) by documents such as invoices, bills, receipts, notes, cash, contracts and written agreements, shipping documents, receiving reports, and paper or digital (computer) statements etc.

It is important to distinguish between personal transactions of the owners, and business transactions on behalf of or by the business as an independent organization (entity) separate from the owners. The business is treated as a separate, non-organic, *person* in the eyes of the law and referred to as a business entity.

Separation of Personal and Business Entity Expenditures and Expenses	
Owner's Personal expenditures/Expenses	**Business Entity Expenditures/Expenses--COA**
Grocery, clothes, travelling, gasoline, rent, telephone, electricity, cable, internet, automobile, mortgage, auto loans, education, entertainment, vacations, personal state and federal taxes etc.	Office and warehouse rental, purchase of inventory for resale, sale of merchandise and services, loans from bank, loan from owner, loan and advances to owners or employees, purchase of office supplies and equipment, insurance, utilities, state and federal taxes, sales taxes, wages and salaries etc.

Business transactions are generally between six main pairs of give/get categories of accounts of a business organization: (1) Assets/Assets (A/ A), (2) Assets/Liabilities (A/ L), (3) Assets/Expenses (A/E), (4) Assets/Revenues (A/R), (5) Liabilities/Expenses (L/E), (6) Assets/Equity (A/OE), or a combination of them. Note that transactions with parties inside or outside of the organization, such as employees, debtors, creditors, banks, and owners, are recorded in the general ledger accounts of the organization (accounts receivable, accounts payable, long-term loans, owner's equity etc.).

SIX PAIRS OF GIVE-GET CATEGORIES OF BUSINESS TRANSACTIONS IN BUSINESS FIRMS					
1. A/A	**2. A/L**	**3. A/E**	**4. A/R**	**5. L/E**	**6. A/OE**
Examples include: FA/Cash, Inventory/Cash, Cash/Receivable	Examples include: Inventory/Payable Cash/Creditors FA/Lenders	Examples include: Cash/Rent, Cash/Insurance Cash/Wages & Sal	Example includes: Cash/Revenue, Receivable/Sales	Examples include: Tax Exp./Payable Ins. Exp./Payable Rent Exp./Payable	Examples include: Cash/OE, Cash/Drawings, FA/OE
FA = Fixed Assets, OE = Owners' Equity, A = Assets, L = Liabilities, E = Expenses, R = Revenue, OE = Owners' Equity					

> **Important:** Only business transactions and activities performed by or on behalf of the business entity are analyzed, recorded, and posted in the books of the business.

The Chart of Accounts (COA)

let us look at the structure of the combined chart of accounts (COA) and trial balance at the end of chapter 1 and imagine moving money (financial transactions) out of (credit) one general ledger account and simultaneously into (debit) another general ledger account. A COA is a list of general ledger accounts set up and used in business firms to identify, record, and post financial transactions conducted on behalf of the organization. Creating and setting up the COA is usually among the first set of activities done by the accountant along with setting up a new bank account for the business.

Notice how the general ledger accounts are numbered and classified in the COA:

- The Balance Sheet (BS) section of the COA contains subcategories listing Asset account numbers beginning with the number 1; Liabilities account numbers starting with the number 2; and Equity account numbers starting with the number 3. The ledger accounts in the balance sheet section are called *permanent* accounts because their balances are carried over from one *financial* period to the next.

- The Income Statement (IS) section of the COA shows subcategories listing Revenue account numbers beginning with the number 4; and Expense account numbers starting with the number 5. The ledger accounts in the income statement section are called *nominal* or *temporary* accounts because their balances are closed out to zero by transferring their totals to an income summary account at the end of each *financial* period. The next financial period begins with zero amounts in these accounts.

- The combined COA and Trial Balance (TB) shows the *normal* types of balances—Debit or Credit, found in accounting systems, as demonstrated by "XXXXXX" in the TB columns, with asset accounts (debit); contra-assets (credit); liabilities (credit); equity accounts (credit); expense accounts (debit); revenue accounts (credit).

The General Journal (GJ)

Steps in The Accounting Process					
STEP 1	STEP 2	STEP 3	STEP 4	STEP 5	STEP 6
Analyze Transactions	Record Journal Entries	Post to General Ledger	Prepare Trial Balance	End-of- Period Adj. Entries	Compile Financial Statements

The chart of accounts (COA) is used to analyze and record business transactions in the journal (see Steps 1 and 2). The general journal is often called the book of first or prime entry because this is where the business transactions are usually first recorded in the books of the firm. Accountants use the COA to aid in analyzing business transactions, to identify the give-get relationship of the transaction, and determine which general ledger is receiving the value (debit) and its source--where the value is coming from (credit). *Journalizing* a transaction is the accounting jargon used to record entries in the journal and involves *debiting*—recording values in the debit section, and *crediting*—recording values in the credit section of the journal. It is important to remember the double-entry concept to ensure the journal balances.

Recall that Master Zen started his company MZ LLC on January 1, 2017, with $20,000.00 equity capital and purchased office equipment for $2,000.00:

General Journal				Page No. 1	
Date 2017		Description	GL Ref.	Debit	Credit
Jan	1	Cash	1010	20,000.00	
		Owner's Capital/Equity	3010		20,000.00
		Master Zen capital investment			
Jan	1	Fixed Assets	1050	2,000.00	
		Cash	1010		2,000.00
		Chk #001 Demp's Office Desks & Chairs			

Notice in the example: the name and page number of the journal; debits are entered on the first line followed by credits in the second line of the entries; the account descriptions (Description) and related account numbers in the GL Ref.; indentation of the second line for the description of the account credited; the debit and credit amounts are equal; explanation of the journal entries are written on a separate line below the entries; and a blank line between the different entries for readability.

Special Journals

Midsize and large organizations usually have several business transactions daily, and it would be cumbersome to record all transactions using general journals containing multiple lines of information and general ledger (GL) account numbers--especially for repetitive types of transactions. Special journals are journals containing pre-numbered GL account numbers across the *top* of the journal, for the GL accounts to be debited along with the corresponding GL accounts to be credited, in single rows for *each* transaction. Five common types of special journals are (1) *Cash Receipts Journal*, in which *all* receipts of cash and checks are recorded; (2) *Cash Payments Journal*—also called *Cash Disbursements Journal*, in which all payments of cash and checks are recorded; (3) *Purchases Journal*, in which non-cash purchases are recorded; (4) *Sales Journal*, in which non-cash sales are recorded; and (5) Payroll Journal, in which salaries and wages of employees are recorded.

The following demonstrate how *general* journals compare to each type of special journal to show the efficiency of using special journals.

Demonstration Examples

1. Purchased books on account, terms, 5/15/N30, from supplier STU $1,500.00 on Invoice #222.
2. Sold books on account, 2/10/N30, to customer CTU $4,000.00 on Invoice #100.
3. Paid invoice #222 $1,500.00 for supplier STU and deducted $75 for 5 percent early payment discount (5 percent of $1,500.00), with check #5 for $1,425.00.
4. Received check #009 for $3,020.00 from customer CTU for full payment of invoice #100 $4,000.00 less early payment discount of $80.00 (2 percent of $4,000.00).
5. Recorded salary and wage expenses for employees for $5,000.00 Gross, and withholdings for federal tax of $750.00 and F.I.C.A of $382.50 (7.65 percent) to be paid at the end of the pay period.

Note: Terms on account 5/15/N30 means that a 5 percent discount can be deducted from the invoice amount if it is paid within 15 days, or the full amount must be paid within 30 days; likewise, 2/10/N30, means 2 percent discount if paid within 10 days, or the invoice amount must be paid in full within 30 days.

The transactions could be recorded in the General Journal *or* the Special Journals using the chart of account as shown in the following tables:

General Journal

Date 20xx		Description	GL Ref.	Debit		Credit	
				Amount		Amount	
	1	Merchandise Inventory	1030	1,500	00		
		Accounts Payable	2010			1,500	00
		Purchase books on account from STU Inv. #222					
	2	Accounts Receivable	1020	4,000	00		
		Sales Revenue	4010			4,000	00
		Sale of Books on account to CTU Inv. # 100					
	3	Accounts Payable	2010	1,500	00		
		Purchases Discount	4031			75	00
		Cash	1010			1,425	00
		Paid chk #5 to STU for Inv. 222 less 5% discount					
	4	Cash	1010	3,020	00		
		Sales Discount	4011	80	00		
		Accounts Receivable	1020			4,000	00
		Chk#009 received from CTU for Inv. #100 less 2%					
	5	Salaries and Wages Expenses	5020	5,000	00		
		Salaries Payable	2020.10			3,867	50
		Federal Income Tax Payable	2020.20			750	00
		F.I.C.A. Payable	2020.30			382	50
		To record salaries and wages expenses for period					

General Journal — Page No. 1

Purchases Journal

Date		Vendor/Supplier	Vendor/Supplier Invoice #	DEBIT Merch. GL AC # 1030 Amount		Other GL ACs GL AC #	Other GL ACs Amount	CREDIT Accounts Payable GL AC # 2010 Subs. AC #	Accounts Payable Amount	
	1	STU	222	1,500	00				1,500	00

Sales Journal

Date		Customer Name	Inv. # or CM #	Subs. AC #	DEBIT Accts. Rec. GL AC # 1020 Amount		CREDIT Sales GL AC # 4010 Amount	
	2	CTU	100		4,000	00	4,000	00

Cash Payments Journal

				DEBIT							CREDIT				
			Accounts Payable GL A/C # 2010		Merch. GL A/C # 1030		Other G/L ACs				Cash GL A/C # 1010		Purch. Disc. GL A/C # 4031		
Date	Chk #	Description	Subs. A/C #	Amount	Amount		G/L A/C #	Amount			Amount		Amount		
3	5	STU			1,500	00					1,425	00	75	00	

Cash Receipts Journal

			DEBIT				CREDIT						
			Cash GL A/C # 1010		Sales Disc. GL A/C # 4011		Accounts Receivable GL A/C # 1020		Sales GL A/C# 4010		Other G/L		
Date	Chk #	Description	Amount		Amount		Subs. A/C #	Amount	Amount		G/L A/C	Amount	
4	009	CTU	3,020	00	80	00		4,000	00				

Payroll Journal

			GROSS PAY DEBIT		FEDERAL DEDUCTIONS CREDIT				SET UP PAYCHECK CREDIT		
			Salaries/Wages GL Expense AC # 5020		Federal Tax GL AC # 2020.20		F.I.C.A. GL AC # 2020.30		Net Pay GL AC # 2020.10		Check Number
Date		Employee Name	Amount		Amount		Amount		Amount		
	5	Misc. Employee names	5,000	00	750	00	382	00	3,867	00	

Think how many lines of entries would be needed in a general journal if there were multiple activities for each type of transaction in a typical week or month, instead of just one or two!

Summary questions of financial activities chapter 2

1) What are the three main tools used in recording and posting transactions in the accounting system of the firm?

a) _____

b) _____

c) _____

2) What kind of transactions are recorded in the journals and posted to the general ledger of the firm?

3) What are the common names given to the activities of recording transactions in the journal, and posting transactions in the general ledger accounts?

Practice Journalizing Transactions 2

Reminder of steps: Each transaction would be recorded on three separate lines: (a) Debit entry, followed by (b) Credit entry, then (c) Explanation for the transaction.

1. Received notice from landlord for unpaid rental of office space for $1,000.00.
2. Received bill from telephone service provider for $130.00 for business telephone service.
3. Bought $2,000.00 books on credit terms from XYZ publishers to sell to customers.
4. Sold $3,500.00 on credit terms to customers.
5. Received invoice for $600.00 for advertising to promote new books with local newspaper to be paid in 30 days.
6. Received electric bill for $530.00 from electric utility company to be paid in 15 days.
7. Purchased office equipment on credit terms from YRU Office Equipment Company for $4,300.00.

Practice Journalizing Transactions using the chart of accounts

1. GL account _____ is DR and GL account _____ is CR for $
2. GL account _____ is DR and GL account _____ is CR for $
3. GL account _____ is DR and GL account _____ is CR for $
4. GL account _____ is DR and GL account _____ is CR for $
5. GL account _____ is DR and GL account _____ is CR for $
6. GL account _____ is DR and GL account _____ is CR for $
7. GL account _____ is DR and GL account _____ is CR for $

Answers to Summary questions of financial activities chapter 2

1) What are the three main tools used in recording and posting transactions in the accounting system of the firm?

    a) The Chart of Accounts (COA)

    b) The Journal

    c) The General Ledger

2) What kind of transactions are recorded in the journals and posted to the general ledger of the firm? Business Transactions.

3) What are the common names given to the acts of recording transactions in the journal, and posting transactions in the general ledger accounts? *Journalizing, debiting,* and *crediting* transactions in the journal and general ledger accounts.

Solutions to Practice Journalizing Transactions using the chart of accounts

1. GL account 5010 is DR and GL account 2010 is CR for $1,000.00
2. GL account 5040 is DR and GL account 2010 is CR for $130.00
3. GL account 1030 is DR and GL account 2010 is CR for $2,000.00
4. GL account 1020 is DR and GL account 4010 is CR for $3,500.00
5. GL account 5060 is DR and GL account 2010 is CR for $600.00
6. GL account 5040 is DR and GL account 2010 is CR for $530.00
7. GL account 1050 is DR and GL account 2010 is CR for $4,300.00

General Journal

General Journal					Page No. 1			
Date 20xx		Description	GL Ref.	Debit		Credit		
				Amount		Amount		
	1	Rent Expense	5010	1,000	00			
		Accounts Payable	2010			1,000	00	
		Office rent due to landlord for office space						
	2	Utilities Expense	5040	130	00			
		Accounts Payable	2010			130	00	
		Telephone service due for period						
	3	Merchandize Inventory	1030	2,000	00			
		Accounts Payable	2010			2,000	00	
		Purchase books on credit from XYZ publishers						

4		Accounts Receivable	1020	3,500	00			
		Sales Revenue	4010				3,500	00
		Sales of books on credit terms						
5		Advertising & Promotion Expense	5060	600	00			
		Accounts Payable	2010				600	00
		Newspaper advertising due local newspaper						
6		Utilities Expense	5040	530	00			
		Accounts Payable	2010				530	00
		Electricity bill due for month						
7		Fixed Asset	1050	4,300	00			
		Accounts Payable	2010				4,300	00
		Purchased office equipment on credit from YRU						

Summary

Accountants use a Chart of Accounts (COA) to record business transactions following the double-entry accounting concept of debits and corresponding credits. Business transactions are first recorded in the journal therefore the journal is often referred to as the book of prime entry. When journalizing transactions, the general ledger accounts receiving value are first recorded (debited), and then the general ledger accounts giving up corresponding (same) values are recorded (credited) on a separate line, thereby ensuring that the journal is in balance.

Cumulative Comprehensive Hands-On Example 2

Let's now trace a few business transactions and look at how they are recorded in the general journal and effects in the Combined Chart of Accounts and Trial Balance of MZ LLC., during the month of January 2017.

Show the journal entries for the following transactions.

- Jan. 1, paid rent for warehouse space to Hoggspace Inc., for the month using check #002 for $1,500.00

- Jan. 2, paid for advertising for the month of January using check #003 to SocMed Adverts LLC., in the amount of $600.00.

- Jan. 4, paid $2,000.00 for 200 books (merchandise inventory) from BooksRU2 Supplies using check #004.

- Jan. 5, Paid insurance premium for the month of January to Firm Status Insurers in the amount of $200.00 on check #005.

- Jan. 6, paid office manager salary of $800.00 for week ending Jan.7, 2017, on check #006.

> Quick note: Whenever you see a transaction with the words *cash* or *paid* you can immediately identify that one of the accounts affected in the journal is the cash account.

Solutions to Cumulative Hands-On Example 2

General Journal			Page No. 1		
Date 2017		Description	GL Ref.	Debit	Credit
Jan	1	Rent Expense	5010	1,500.00	
		Cash	1010		1,500.00
		Chk #002 Hoggspace Inc. Whse. rent Jan.			
Jan	2	Advertising & Promotion	5060	600.00	
		Cash	1010		600.00
		Chk #003 SocMed Adverts Jan. advertising			
Jan	4	Merchandise Inventory	1030	2,000.00	
		Cash	1010		2,000.00
		Chk #004 BooksRU2 Supplies 200 books			
Jan	5	Insurance Expense	5050	200.00	
		Cash	1010		200.00
		Chk #005 Firm Status Ins. Ins. prem Jan			
Jan	6	Salaries & Wages	5020	800.00	
		Cash	1010		800.00
		Chk #006 Office manager salary W/E Jan. 07			

A Simple Combined Chart of Accounts and Trial Balance, MZ LLC 01/07/2017

CHART OF ACCOUNTS	TRIAL BALANCE	
Account #, Classification, and General Ledger Descriptions	Debit $$	Credit $$
Balance Sheet		
Assets: 1000		
• 1010 Cash	12,900.00	
• 1020 Accounts Receivable	XXXX.XX	
• 1021 Allowance for Bad Debts		XXXX.XX
• 1030 Merchandise Inventory	2,000.00	
• 1040 Prepaid Accounts	XXXX.XX	
• 1050 Fixed Assets	2,000.00	
• 1051 Accumulated Depreciation		XXXX.XX
Liabilities: 2000		
• 2010 Accounts Payable		XXXX.XX
• 2020 Wages & Salaries Payable		XXXX.XX
• 2030 Long-term Payable		XXXX.XX
• 2040 Unearned Revenue		XXXX.XX
Equity: 3000		
• 3010 Owner's Capital/Equity		20,000.00
• 3020 Drawing	XXXX.XX	
• 3030 Retained Earnings		XXXX.XX
Income Statement		
Revenue: 4000		
• 4010 Sales Revenue		XXXX.XX
• 4020 Other Revenue		XXXX.XX
• 4030 Cost of Goods Sold (COGS)	XXXX.XX	
Expenses: 5000		
• 5010 Rent Expense	1,500.00	
• 5020 Salaries & Wages	800.00	
• 5030 Office Expenses & Supplies	XXXX.XX	
• 5040 Utilities Expense	XXXX.XX	
• 5050 Insurance Expense	200.00	
• 5060 Advertising & Promotion Expense	600.00	
• 5070 Depreciation Expense	XXXX.XX	
• 5080 Vehicle, Travelling & Entertainment Expense	XXXX.XX	
• 5090 Miscellaneous Expense	XXXX.XX	
	$20,000.00	$20,000.00

(right margin, vertical labels: BALANCE SHEET / INCOME STATEMENT)

Chapter 3: The General Ledger and the Trial Balance

The General Ledger (GL)

Steps in The Accounting Process					
STEP 1	**STEP 2**	**STEP 3**	**STEP 4**	**STEP 5**	**STEP 6**
Analyze Transactions	Record Journal Entries	Post to General Ledger	Prepare Trial Balance	End-of Period Adj. Entries	Compile Financial Statements

Question: What is the purpose of this chapter?

Answer: Provide an overview of the makeup of a typical accounting system using general ledger accounts.

The general ledger contains all the firm's ledger accounts listed on the chart of accounts (COA). Business transactions are *posted* to the individual ledger accounts from the entries recorded in the journal on the same sides as recorded in the journal, and the balances in the ledger accounts updated immediately. This type of immediate updating of the general ledger account balances are called *perpetual* updating, as shown in the tables below.

Journal entries relating to general ledger accounts are sometimes totaled and posted *periodically* (weekly or monthly) as one entry in the account instead of individually. Individual postings to the related general ledger accounts recorded in the journal for the first week of January 2017, are as shown in the following tables, notice the perpetually updated balances:

General Ledger						
Account Name: Cash				**Account No.: 1010**		
				Post JL here		Updated Balance	
Date 2017		**Trans. Description**	**JL Ref.**	**Debit**	**Credit**	**Debit**	**Credit**
Jan.	1	General Journal	J1	20,000.00		20,000.00	
Jan.	1	General Journal	J1		2,000.00	18,000.00	
Jan.	1	General Journal	J1		1,500.00	16,500.00	
Jan.	2	General Journal	J1		600.00	15,900.00	
Jan.	4	General Journal	J1		2,000.00	13,900.00	
Jan.	5	General Journal	J1		200.00	13,700.00	
Jan.	6	General Journal	J1		800.00	12,900.00	

General Ledger

Account Name: Merchandise Inventory **Account No.: 1030**

Date 2017		Trans. Description	JL Ref.	Post JL here Debit	Credit	Updated Balance Debit	Credit
Jan.	4	General Journal	J1	2,000.00		2,000.00	

General Ledger

Account Name: Fixed Assets **Account No.: 1050**

Date 2017		Trans. Description	JL Ref.	Post JL here Debit	Credit	Updated Balance Debit	Credit
Jan.	1	General Journal	J1	2,000.00		2,000.00	

General Ledger

Account Name: Owner's Capital/Equity **Account No.: 3010**

Date 2017		Trans. Description	JL Ref.	Post JL here Debit	Credit	Updated Balance Debit	Credit
Jan.	1	General Journal	J1		20,000.00		20,000.00

General Ledger

Account Name: Rent Expense **Account No.: 5010**

Date 2017		Trans. Description	JL Ref.	Post JL here Debit	Credit	Updated Balance Debit	Credit
Jan.	1	General Journal	J1	1,500.00		1,500.00	

General Ledger

Account Name: Salaries & Wages **Account No.: 5020**

Date 2017		Trans. Description	JL Ref.	Post JL here Debit	Credit	Updated Balance Debit	Credit
Jan.	6	General Journal	J1	800.00		800.00	

General Ledger

Account Name: Insurance Expense **Account No.: 5050**

Date 2017		Trans. Description	JL Ref.	Post JL here Debit	Credit	Updated Balance Debit	Credit
Jan.	5	General Journal	J1	200.00		200.00	

General Ledger							
Account Name: Advertising & Promotion						Account No.: 5060	
				Post JL here		Updated Balance	
Date 2017		Trans. Description	JL Ref.	Debit	Credit	Debit	Credit
Jan.	2	General Journal	J1	600.00		600.00	

Please note the following in the previous general ledger account examples:

- The dates are the same as on the General Journal.

- The *Trans. Description* section refers to the type of journal—the general journal. This is used when there are large numbers of transactions during the period. Some accountants may use the name of the corresponding account instead to identify the other account involved in the transaction and the explanation provided for the journal entry. For example, the *Trans. Description* column in the preceding Cash ledger account might show instead of *General Journal* on January 1: *Owner's Capital/Equity*; *Fixed Assets*; and *Rent Expense* respectively for the first three lines of entries.

- The JL Ref. section indicates the page number shown at the top of the General Journal containing the transactions, in this case page 1.

- The amounts are posted in the general ledger account in the *same* columns, debit or credit as shown in the General Journal for the account in the "Post JL here" section.

- The "Updated Balance" section shows the latest balance in the ledger accounts *after* each transaction is posted—also called the perpetual balance of the account. Notice in the case of the Cash account, the debit of $10,000.00 increased the *debit* balance in the account on January 1, while the subsequent *credits reduced* the balance remaining in the account.

> **Asset and Expense accounts normally have debit balances that are reducible by credit entries; Liability, Equity, and Revenue accounts normally have credit balances that are reducible by debit entries.**

Chapter 3: The General Ledger and the Trial Balance
The Trial Balance (TB)

Steps in The Accounting Process					
STEP 1	STEP 2	STEP 3	STEP 4	STEP 5	STEP 6
Analyze Transactions	Record Journal Entries	Post to General Ledger	Prepare Trial Balance	End-of Period Adj. Entries	Compile Financial Statements

A Trial Balance (TB) is a tool used by accountants to verify that the total general ledger accounts with debit balances are equal in total to the accounts with credit balances; accounts with zero balances are generally not shown on a TB. The TB does not verify the accuracy of the postings or amounts; only that the total debits equal the total credits of the accounts in the general ledger.

As demonstrated in the Combined Chart of Accounts and Trial Balance shown throughout the book, the TB is a list showing all general ledger accounts and their current balances. The debit column of the TB is totaled at the bottom—called *footing* and compared with the total of the credit column to verify equality (comparison is referred to as *cross-footing* the columns).

If the total amounts do not match, the accountant must locate and correct the reason(s) for the mismatch. This is done by first identifying the difference between the two totals to see if an amount is omitted, posted on the wrong column, or divisible by the number 9 which could indicate a transposition of an amount in the TB. Otherwise, it might be necessary to review and confirm that all journal entries have been recorded and posted correctly in the general ledger accounts in accordance with the double-entry concept.

Even if the total debits and credits cross-foot—have equal amounts, the trial balance (TB) does not confirm that the amounts are correct or correctly posted to the right accounts, as this is not the purpose of the TB; only that the total debit balances equal the total credit balances. If a check is paid to a supplier for $900.00 and is incorrectly recorded in the journal and posted to the general ledger as $90.00, the TB would still be in balance though the records are incorrect. Or, if an amount paid for rent is recorded and posted to insurance expense in error it would not be immediately identified as incorrect in the TB.

Summary

Business transactions are originally recorded in the general journal in accordance with the chart of accounts (COA) of the firm and the double-entry concept of accounting. The journal entries are then transferred—posted to related general ledger accounts and balances are updated to include the latest transactions. The current, updated (perpetual) balances of the general ledger accounts are listed in a trial balance (TB), a tool showing the list of general accounts and balances used by accountants to verify and confirm that the total of accounts with debit balances are equal to the total of accounts with credit balances. The TB only confirms the double-entry accounting concept that total debits equals total credits in the general ledger account balances.

Chapter 3: The General Ledger and the Trial Balance

Summary questions of financial activities chapter 3

1) Using the Chart of Accounts (COA), indicate in which general ledger account number (GL#); and financial statement, balance sheet (BS) or income statement (IS), you would find the following transactions (account DR and financial statement, then account CR and financial statement):

   a) Investment of cash by owner to start the business.

   b) Cash purchase of office desks and chairs.

   c) Payment of warehouse rental.

   d) Payment for advertising.

   e) Cash purchase of books (merchandise).

   f) Payment of insurance premium.

   g) Payment of salaries and wages.

Practice Journalizing Transactions 3

Reminder of steps: Each transaction would be recorded on three separate lines: (a) Debit entry, followed by (b) Credit entry, then (c) Explanation for the transaction.

   1. Paid check for $6,000.00 to landlord in advance 6 month's rent of office space.

   2. Borrowed $10,000.00 from the bank on a long-term note to be repaid in 5 years.

   3. Journalized the $1,500.00 cost to the firm (purchase) of the books that were sold to customers to reduce the remaining value (cost) of inventory on the books.

   4. Received $2,500.00 in advance for pre-orders from customers for upcoming editions of books to be delivered in 3 months.

   5. Paid insurance in advance of $2,400 for 2 years of liability insurance coverage.

   6. Spent $250 on business expenses--travelling and entertainment with customers.

   7. Paid $100.00 for office supplies from Papers 'N Stuff supplies.

Practice Journalizing Transactions using the chart of accounts

   1. GL account _____ is DR and GL account _____ is CR for $

   2. GL account _____ is DR and GL account _____ is CR for $

   3. GL account _____ is DR and GL account _____ is CR for $

   4. GL account _____ is DR and GL account _____ is CR for $

   5. GL account _____ is DR and GL account _____ is CR for $

   6. GL account _____ is DR and GL account _____ is CR for $

   7. GL account _____ is DR and GL account _____ is CR for $

Answers to Summary questions of financial activities chapter 3

1) Using the Chart of Accounts (COA), indicate in which general ledger account number (GL#); and financial statement, balance sheet (BS) or income statement (IS), you would find the following transactions (account DR and financial statement, then account CR and financial statement):

a) Investment of cash by owner to start the business: GL# 1010 (BS), GL#3010 (BS).

b) Cash purchase of office desks and chairs: GL# 1050 (BS), GL#1010 (BS).

c) Payment of warehouse rental: GL# 5010 (IS), GL#1010 (BS).

d) Payment for advertising: GL# 5060 (IS), GL#1010 (BS).

e) Cash purchase of books (merchandise): GL# 1030 (BS), GL#1010 (BS).

f) Payment of insurance premium: GL# 5050 (IS), GL#1010 (BS).

g) Payment of salaries and wages: GL# 5020 (IS), GL#1010 (BS).

Solutions to Practice Journalizing Transactions using the chart of accounts

1. GL account <u>1040</u> is DR and GL account <u>1010</u> is CR for $6,000.00
2. GL account <u>1010</u> is DR and GL account <u>2030</u> is CR for $10,000.00
3. GL account <u>4030</u> is DR and GL account <u>1030</u> is CR for $1,500.00
4. GL account <u>1010</u> is DR and GL account <u>2040</u> is CR for $2,500.00
5. GL account <u>1040</u> is DR and GL account <u>1010</u> is CR for $2,400.00
6. GL account <u>5080</u> is DR and GL account <u>1010</u> is CR for $250.00
7. GL account <u>5030</u> is DR and GL account <u>1010</u> is CR for $100.00

General Journal

		General Journal			Debit		Page No. 1	
Date 20xx		Description	GL Ref.	Debit		Credit		
				Amount		Amount		
	1	Prepaid Accounts-Rental	1040	6,000	00		
		Cash	1010			6,000	00
		Advance payment of 6 month's rent for office space					
	2	Cash	1010	10,000	00		
		Long-term Payable	2030			10,000	00
		Note payable for loan from bank					
	3	Cost of Goods Sold	4030	1,500	00		
		Merchandise Inventory	1030			1,500	00
		Cost of books that were sold					

	4	Cash	1010	2,500	00		
		Unearned Revenue	2040			2,500	00
		Pre-order cash received from customers					
	5	Prepaid Accounts-Insurance	1040	2,400	00		
		Cash	1010			2,400	00
		Advance payment for 2 years liability insurance					
	6	Vehicle, Travelling & Entertainment Expense	5080	250	00		
		Cash	1010			250	00
		Business expenses for entertaining customers					
	7	Office Expense & Supplies	5030	100	00		
		Cash	1010			100	00
		Misc. office supplies purchased and expensed					

Cumulative Comprehensive Hands-on Example 3

Show the Trial Balance of MZ LLC as at January 7, 2017.

Solutions to Cumulative Hands-On Example 3

A Simple Combined Chart of Accounts and Trial Balance, MZ LLC 01/07/2017		
CHART OF ACCOUNTS	**TRIAL BALANCE**	
Account #, Classification, and General Ledger Descriptions	**Debit $$**	**Credit $$**
Balance Sheet		
Assets: 1000		
• 1010 Cash	12,900.00	
• 1030 Merchandise Inventory	2,000.00	
• 1050 Fixed Assets	2,000.00	
Equity: 3000		
• 3010 Owner's Capital/Equity		20,000.00
Income Statement		
Expenses: 5000		
• 5010 Rent Expense	1,500.00	
• 5020 Salaries & Wages	800.00	
• 5050 Insurance Expense	200.00	
• 5060 Advertising & Promotion Expense	600.00	
	$20,000.00	$20,000.00

(Side labels: BALANCE SHEET, INCOME STATEMENT)

Chapter 4: Elements of The Balance Sheet
Chapter 4: Elements of The Balance Sheet
The Balance Sheet (BS)

Steps in The Accounting Process					
__STEP 1__	__STEP 2__	__STEP 3__	__STEP 4__	__STEP 5__	__STEP 6__
Analyze Transactions	Record Journal Entries	Post to General Ledger	Prepare Trial Balance	End-of Period Adj. Entries	Compile Financial Statements

Question: What is the purpose of this chapter?

Answer: To identify the permanent accounts in the chart of accounts used in the balance sheet.

The balance sheet summarizes what the organization owns—Assets; what it owes to others—Liabilities; and what is owed to owners of the organization—Equity at the end of a financial period. The balance sheet displays the *Accounting Equation*: Asset = Liability – Equity in detail. We will delay the completion of the balance sheet statement until chapter 6 after closing entries are posted to the income summary account and the net profit or loss for the firm is determined and reported in the income statement report.

In defining the chart of accounts (COA) in chapter 2, general ledger accounts that make up the balance sheet were described as *permanent* accounts because their balances are carried over from one *financial* period to the next. A review of the *Simple Combined Chart of Accounts and Trial Balance* at the end of previous chapters and in Appendix A, shows the categories, description and account numbers that make up the *elements* of the balance sheet. The COA shows the following subcategories: Asset account numbers beginning with number 1; Liabilities account numbers beginning with the number 2; and Equity account numbers, the number 3.

Notice that the chart of accounts (COA) was designed to hold up to 999 different general ledger accounts in each subcategory. The Assets subcategory was designed to accommodate account numbers between 1000 and 1999; the Liability section 2000 to 2999, and the Equities section 3000 to 3999.

Assets

Assets are physical and other valuable resources owned by the organization to be used to support the objectives of the organization. The assets subcategory is generally subdivided into current assets, long-term assets, and intangible assets (not included in this COA). Asset accounts in the general ledger normally have *debit* balances and the number of asset subcategories listed in the balance sheet depends on the reporting requirements of the kind and size of the organization. Many public organizations have many subcategories to provide additional detail to users of the financial statements for decision making and comparative analyses of the organization with other financial periods, or with other organizations and competitors.

Assets are reported on the balance sheet in the order of liquidity, from most liquid to least liquid, with the most liquid asset being cash. The liquidity of an asset refers to how quickly the asset can be converted to cash.

Current Assets

Current assets are expected to be used up within the normal operating cycle of the organization, or one year whichever is more. Most operating periods of organizations are calendar years such as January to December, or other 12—month periods, such as March to the following February. The following are just a few popular classifications of current assets used in most retail organizations.

- *Cash and Cash Equivalents* are money in the bank account, cash on hand, and petty cash. Cash equivalents are things like certificates of deposit and treasury bills that can be easily converted into specific sums of money on short notice as needed.

- *Accounts Receivable* are amounts owed *to* the firm by customers to whom goods were sold on terms—on credit and are still unpaid at the date of the balance sheet. These are non-cash customers allowed to purchase and own the items immediately with the agreement to pay for them later, such as in 30 days from the date of the invoice. The journal entry for recording *sales on terms* to customers is to debit the accounts receivable account for the amounts unpaid—owed *by* customers and credit to the sales or revenue account. *Cash sales* are debited directly to the cash account and credited to sales revenue; no accounts receivable is involved because customers paid in cash and do not owe the firm for these transactions.

- *Allowance for Bad Debts*, also called allowance for doubtful accounts, are amounts in the balance of the accounts receivable that are estimated by the accountant will not be paid by customers when they are due. They are indirectly written off against income for the period. The journal entry to record the estimated bad debt is: debit Bad Debt Expense account and credit the Allowance for Bad Debts account. The balance in this account is a negative (credit) amount, and the account is called a contra-asset account because assets normally have debit balances. Notice that the contra-asset account is a subset of the related asset account in the COA. The amount estimated in the allowance for bad debt account is subtracted from the outstanding amount shown for accounts receivable on the balance sheet to show the *net* accounts receivable expected to be collectible on the date of the balance sheet.

- *Merchandise Inventory* are items purchased by retailers and wholesalers from suppliers, also called vendors, to sell to customers with little or no modification to make a profit. These are not items purchased to be used as supplies for the office or warehouse of the firm, but products to resell to customer in regular business operations.

Inventory for a firm represents the main "products" the firm sells to its customers, whether the product is a finished item such as a car, or car parts. A car dealer, for instance, might sell both cars and car parts; both are merchandise inventory for the car dealer. Service type organizations do not generally have merchandise accounts because their main *product* is the *service* or expertise they provide for a fee, although some might also sell parts to customers. The journal to record the purchase of merchandise inventory is: debit Merchandise Inventory account, and credit cash (if paid immediately) or credit Accounts Payable if purchased on terms—credit.

Recall in chapter 2 that MZ LLC purchased 200 books at a *cost* of $10.00 each, totaling $2,000.00, for merchandise inventory. The organization sells the books at a higher sales price at a *markup*, by adding an amount to the cost of each book, called *profit margin*. Hence the selling price (cost plus profit margin) of the books to customers is greater than the amount paid by MZ LLC for the books.

Before finishing the discussion on inventory, I will briefly introduce three cost assumptions—cost concepts of inventory cost which are matched to the related sales for the period on the income statement: First in First out (FIFO); Last in First Out (LIFO); and Weighted average. These are cost assumptions made by accountants to determine gross profit made on revenue (sales) for a specific period; especially when prices for merchandise changes frequently and the firm must pay different prices at different dates for *similar* items.

As an example, suppose that MZ LLC purchases additional books as follows: Jan. 8, 25 books for $12.00 each, totaling $300.00; Jan. 16, 25 books at $9.00, each totaling $225.00; and Jan. 21, 50 books at $8.00 each for a total amount of $400.00. The total cost of the 300 books in inventory available for sale for the period January 1, to January 21, would be $2,925.00 (2,000.00 + 300.00 + 225.00 + 400.00).

If MZ LLC also sold 150 books at $60.00 each (sales price of the firm) during the same period, total revenue would be $9,000.00 (150 x 60.00). The inventory balance at the end of the period is therefore 150 units (200 + 25 + 25 + 50 − 150).

How would the matching cost be determined under each cost flow assumption? Notice there are four different cost layers: $10.00 (Jan. 1), $12.00 (Jan. 8), $9.00 (Jan. 16), and $8.00 (Jan. 21). The valuations shown in the following diagrams are based on the *periodic* costing method of valuing the inventory remaining at the end of the period Jan. 21, 2017, with amounts expensed to C.O.S. in the lighter areas indicated, with the remainder in the inventory account.

COST OF INVENTORY AVAILABLE FOR SALE				
	JAN. 1	JAN. 8	JAN. 16	JAN. 21
Purch. Unit/cost	200 @ $10.00	25 @ $12.00	25 @ $9.00	50 $8.00
Purchase cost	$2,000.00	$300.00	$225.00	$400.00
Cumulative total	200 $2,000.00	225 $2,300.00	250 $2,525.00	300 $2,925.00

FIFO Inventory value ending balance $1,425.00 and COS $1,500.00

INVENTORY VALUE & COS UNDER FIRST-IN-FIRST-OUT AFTER SALE OF 150 UNITS					
	JAN. 1	JAN. 1	JAN. 8	JAN. 16	JAN. 21
Purch. Unit/cost	150 @ $10.00	50 @ $10.00	25 @ $12.00	25 @ $9.00	50 $8.00
Purchase cost	$1,500.00	$500.00	$300.00	$225.00	$400.00
Cumulative total	150 $1,500.00	50 $500.00	75 $800.00	100 $1,025.00	150 $1,425.00

LIFO Inventory value ending balance $1,500.00 and COS $1,425.00

INVENTORY VALUE & COS UNDER LAST-IN-FIRST-OUT AFTER SALE OF 150 UNITS					
	JAN. 1	JAN. 1	JAN. 8	JAN. 16	JAN. 21
Purch. Unit/cost	150 @ $10.00	50 @ $10.00	25 @ $12.00	25 @ $9.00	50 $8.00
Purchase cost	$1,500.00	$500.00	$300.00	$225.00	$400.00
Cumulative total	150 $1,500.00	50 $500.00	75 $800.00	100 $1,025.00	150 $1,425.00

Average Cost Inventory value ending balance $1,462.50 and COS $1,462.50 (150 x 9.75).

PERIODIC INVENTORY UNIT AVERAGE COST				
	JAN. 1	JAN. 8	JAN. 16	JAN. 21	JAN. 21
Purch. Unit/cost	200 @ $10.00	25 @ $12.00	25 @ $9.00	50 $8.00	
Purchase cost	$2,000.00	$300.00	$225.00	$400.00	
Periodic Average		Total cost/Total Units $2,925.00/300			9.75 each

Long-Term Assets

Long-term assets are expected to be useful to the firm for more than a year and expensed over a period calculated to match revenues directly or indirectly generated by such assets. As with current assets, the number of fixed asset classification will vary depending on the size and scope of the organization. General classifications may include office buildings, office furniture and equipment, computer equipment, land, vehicles, warehouse equipment etc.

Chapter 4: Elements of The Balance Sheet

- *Fixed Assets* are bought to be used by the firm to support the operations of the business over a long period of time—a year or more. Although not immediately obvious to the new learner, the costs of fixed assets will eventually be expensed as part of the operating cost of the business in generating revenues and profits. The initial historical costs of the fixed assets are not expensed immediately in the income statement but spread over current and future operating periods benefitting from the usage of the assets. The operating efficiency of fixed assets deteriorate over time, and some, such as computer equipment, may become outdated or obsolete quickly because of the introduction of new, more efficient technology. The recorded historical costs of fixed assets are reduced—expensed against periodic revenues over time, by a process called depreciation. The historical original purchase price paid for the asset is maintained in the general ledger account and netted against the accumulated depreciation account, a *contra-asset* account with a negative value (credit), to show the reduced or net value of the long-term asset on the balance sheet.

  As described earlier in relation to the account for doubtful account, a contra-asset account carries a negative—credit value in the assets section of the balance sheet instead of the normal, positive, debit values. Notice that this contra-asset account is a subset of the account to which it is related in the chart of accounts. Fixed assets transactions are recorded in the journal by debiting the Fixed Assets account and crediting Cash (if paid for immediately) or credit Long-Term Payable, if payment is postponed for a future date—on terms.

- *Accumulated Depreciation* is the *contra-asset* in the balance sheet for the credit side of the depreciation expense recorded in the income statement to depreciate long-term assets. Depreciation expense is based on estimates for the useful productive life (time) or usage (production) of the related assets, and the calculated amount is debited to the depreciation expense account and credited, not to the long-term asset account, but to the related accumulated depreciation account. The account is called accumulated because it contains the total amount of depreciation expense to the related asset since the date of its purchase.

  Two bases used by accountants to estimate depreciation expense for fixed assets are (1) time, straight-line (most popular) or modified, in number of years; and (2) units of production for a manufacturer such as maximum estimated number of units that can potentially be produced by a machine, or total estimated production hours of usage.

(1) An example of depreciation based on time is straight line depreciation: the value of the asset (the historical price paid less a residual or disposal value) divided by an estimated number of years of useful life such as 5 years. For instance, if a machine was purchased for $5,000.00 with estimated useful life of 5 years and residual value of $1,000.00, the yearly straight-line depreciation would be calculated as $4,000.00 ($5,000.00 - $1,000.00) divided by 5 (yrs.) or $4,000.00/5 = $800.00 per year journalized by debiting depreciation expense account $800.00 and crediting accumulated depreciation—machinery $800.00.

(2) The second depreciation basis used in a manufacturing firm is related to usage of the machine, such as on total number of units to be produced or total estimated production hours, over the useful life of the asset. For instance, if the machine described in the previous section was estimated to produce 40,000 units over its productive life, the depreciation expense would be based on $0.10 per unit of production ($4,000.00 / 40,000). If the number of units produced on the machine *for a period* is 5,000 then the depreciation expense (debit) and accumulated depreciation (credit) amount would be $500.00 (5,000 x $0.10 per unit).

- *Intangible Assets* are not covered in this book or in the chart of accounts (COA). These are assets that cannot be physically touched—intangible but are of economic value to the firm such as copyrights, patents, trade-marks and goodwill.

Liabilities

Liabilities are debts for goods and services incurred by or on behalf of the organization that remain unpaid at the date of the balance sheet. Examples of liabilities include: debts for unpaid merchandise purchased on terms—on credit by the firm; unpaid services provided by employees or other individuals and firms; amounts owed to utility providers; and unpaid amounts due to government agencies. Liability accounts in the general ledger normally contain *credit* balance amounts with categories in the balance sheet subdivided into current liabilities and long-term Liabilities, including unearned Revenue. The different types and numbers of liability accounts and subcategories depend on the operating and reporting needs of the organization and set up in the chart of accounts. Some organizations will have a variety of

Chapter 4: Elements of The Balance Sheet

subcategories for more in-depth analyses to more accurately report on the status and activities of the organization.

Current Liabilities

Like current assets, current liabilities (short-term debts owed by the organization) are expected to be paid within one year or the normal operating cycle of the organization whichever is longer. The operating cycle, also called fiscal year, of organizations can be a calendar year such as January to December, or other 12—month periods, such as March to the following February. Some popular classifications (elements) of current liabilities or debts used by retail organizations are:

- *Accounts Payable* represents operating debts owed by the organization to third parties for goods and services provided to the firm and are expected to be paid in the current fiscal year. One of the largest amounts in this category for retailers and wholesalers are transactions related to the purchase of merchandise inventory from suppliers and vendors on terms—credit. Amounts usually found in this category could include amounts unpaid for utilities, taxes and licenses payable to government agencies, and amounts owed for other operating and office supplies. The journal entry to record an accounts payable transaction is debit the relevant asset or expense account and credit the Accounts Payable account.

- *Salaries & Wages Payable* is a special category for unpaid amounts owed to employees for work performed for the organization. This is a normal category in business because employees are usually paid weekly, bi-weekly, or monthly *after* their services are provided to the firm. In other words, wages and salaries will usually be outstanding— owed to employees at any time for services provided to the organization to be paid on the next payday. This is also called *accrued* wages and salaries. The journal entry to record unpaid salaries and wages, is debit the Salaries & Wages *Expense* account, and credit the Salaries & Wages *Payable* account.

  Employers responsible for withholding certain *statutory* amounts from the wages and salaries of employees on behalf of city, state, and/or federal governments, to be paid over to the government at specific periods. Statutory *employee* withholding amounts include Social Security and Medicare (F.I.C.A.) and Federal Income Tax and may be grouped and shown separately on the balance sheet. Additionally, statutory *employer* tax amounts are additionally owed to the government by firms for federal unemployment taxes (F.U.T.A.) and state unemployment taxes (S.U.T.A.) and shown in the balance sheet.

Long-Term Liabilities

Long-term liabilities are debts incurred by the firm which are agreed to be repaid in over a year—beyond the current fiscal period. These are debts usually incurred to purchase big-ticket items such as buildings, office furniture and equipment, and operating machinery. Long-term liabilities may also include large amounts of cash borrowed to help finance the operations of the firm for several years. Long-term liabilities for large sums of money are generally secured by a mortgage note (land and buildings) or long-term notes payable (furniture and equipment, operating machinery, automobile and trucks etc.), and may also require personal guarantees by owners of the firm to repay the loan when due, especially in small firms.

- *Long-Term Payable* classification is used for debts or loans that are not due to be repaid within the fiscal year. These debts are usually secured by resources of the company and carry interest charges payable in the current period, such as monthly or quarterly and principal payments paid in installments or a lump sum at a specific time in the future. The periodic payments might include amounts for interest *and* reduction of the unpaid debt. The journal entries to record a transaction for long-term debt is generally a debit to Assets (Cash or Fixed Assets) and credit a Long-term Payable account.

- *Unearned Revenue* is not a long-term liability as such, but could be classified as long-term, if customers pay in advance for goods or services to be provided over a year later. Whenever customers pay for goods or services to be received in the future, the firm does not *earn* the related revenues until the goods or services are delivered to the customer—until ownership of the goods passes to the customer. Since the organization has not yet *earned* the revenue, the journal to record such a transaction is to debit the Cash account for the amount advances and credit the Unearned Revenue account.

Equity

The Equity subcategory of the balance sheet is usually subdivided into Owner's Capital, Drawings, and Retained Earnings.

- *Owner's Capital/Equity* represents cash or other resources invested by owners to start and finance the operations of the business as a separate entity. Additional capital resources invested in the business by the owner could include items such as machinery and equipment, office furniture and equipment, merchandise, land and building and trucks or automobiles etc. Journal entries to record the capital resources initially invested in the business by the owner are usually done at the start of the new entity. Additional entries to the account would be recorded if the owners provided additional resources to the business in the future. The journal entries to record these transactions usually involve debits to appropriate asset accounts (such as Cash or Office Furniture) and corresponding credit to the Owner's Capital/Equity account. The transaction is also called *capitalizing* the firm.

- *Drawings* represent *withdrawal* of cash or other resources *from* the business for personal use by owners of the firm, thereby reducing the overall Equity balance of the firm. When an owner withdraws cash or assets from the business for personal use, the related asset account is credited for the reduction, and the Drawings account is debited for the value withdrawn. The Drawing account is a *contra-equity* account because it carries a debit balance against the normal credit balances of the equity accounts on the balance sheet.

- *Retained Earnings* general ledger account contains the accumulated (current and previous) net income or loss amounts of prior and current operating periods not distributed to the owners. At the end of each fiscal period the net income from the Income Statement (Income Summary account) is closed out to the Retained Earnings account.

Expenditure and Expense

A quick note on the usage of the terms, expenditure and expense: Accountants refer to the actual spending of cash to purchase or pay for something by the business as an *expenditure*, whereas *expensing* of an amount refers to the allocation of the amount to the expense section of the income statement. For instance, the purchase of an office desk for cash is considered expenditure and reported in the balance sheet, while the periodic depreciation—writing off the cost of the desk in the income statement over time is considered expensing it.

Summary

This chapter provided an overview of the basic structure of an accounting system and general classification, subsections, and elements (accounts) of a typical balance sheet. The accounts are briefly described to provide understanding of how they are used in the business environment and within organizations.

Summary questions of financial activities chapter 4

1) Using the Chart of Accounts (COA), indicate in which general ledger account number (GL#); and financial statement, balance sheet (BS) or income statement (IS), you would find the following transactions (account DR and financial statement, then account CR and financial statement):

   a) Sold books on account (credit terms) to customer A who promises to pay in 30 days.

   b) Purchased books for inventory (merchandise for resale) on credit terms (on account) from vendor.

   c) Recorded rental expense for month to be paid next period.

   d) Received loan from bank to be repaid in 7 years and signed a promissory note payable.

   e) Recorded salary expense for office manager to be paid bi-weekly in next pay period.

   f) Received advance deposits for pre-paid sale of books from customers to be delivered in 4 months.

   g) Leased vehicle from car dealership to make deliveries and paid for lease in cash.

Practice Journalizing Transactions 4

Reminder of steps: Each transaction would be recorded on three separate lines: (a) Debit entry, followed by (b) Credit entry, then (c) Explanation for the transaction.

   1. Received check for $2,000.00 from credit customers on account for prior sales.
   2. Paid $1,200 on account to book vendors for prior purchases of inventory.
   3. Paid past due rent of $1,000.00 for prior period previously expensed in GL.
   4. Paid interest due on long-term loan to bank and recorded pmt to Office Expenses $200.
   5. Paid check for $2,400.00 bi-weekly salary to office manager previously recorded in GL.
   6. Delivered $2,300 books to pre-paid customers and moved amount to Sales Revenue.
   7. Recorded monthly payment of $500 for lease of small truck from dealership.

Practice Journalizing Transactions using the chart of accounts

   1. GL account _____ is DR and GL account _____ is CR for $
   2. GL account _____ is DR and GL account _____ is CR for $
   3. GL account _____ is DR and GL account _____ is CR for $
   4. GL account _____ is DR and GL account _____ is CR for $
   5. GL account _____ is DR and GL account _____ is CR for $
   6. GL account _____ is DR and GL account _____ is CR for $
   7. GL account _____ is DR and GL account _____ is CR for $

Chapter 4: Elements of The Balance Sheet

Answers to Summary questions of financial activities chapter 4

1) Using the Chart of Accounts (COA), indicate in which general ledger account number (GL#); and financial statement, balance sheet (BS) or income statement (IS), you would find the following transactions (account DR and financial statement, then account CR and financial statement):

a) Sold books on account (credit terms) to customer A: GL# 1020 (BS), GL#4010 (IS).

b) Purchased books for inventory on credit terms: GL# 1030 (BS), GL#2010 (BS).

c) Recorded rental expense for month not paid: GL# 5010 (IS), GL#2010 (BS).

d) Received loan from bank to be repaid in 7 years: GL# 1010 (BS), GL#2030 (BS).

e) Recorded unpaid salary expense for office manager: GL# 5020 (IS), GL#2020 (BS).

f) Received advance deposits for pre-paid sale of books: GL# 1010 (BS), GL#2040 (BS).

g) Leased vehicle from car dealership, paid in cash: GL# 5080 (IS), GL#1010 (BS).

Solutions to Practice Journalizing Transactions using the chart of accounts

1. GL account 1010 is DR and GL account 1020 is CR for $2,000.00
2. GL account 2010 is DR and GL account 1010 is CR for $1,200.00
3. GL account 2010 is DR and GL account 1010 is CR for $1,000.00
4. GL account 5030 is DR and GL account 1010 is CR for $200.00
5. GL account 2020 is DR and GL account 1010 is CR for $2,400.00
6. GL account 2040 is DR and GL account 4010 is CR for $2,300.00
7. GL account 5080 is DR and GL account 1010 is CR for $500.00

General Journal

		General Journal				Page No. 1	
Date 20xx		Description	GL Ref.	Debit		Credit	
				Amount		Amount	
	1	Cash	1010	2,000	00		
		Accounts Receivable	1020			2,000	00
		Check received on account from credit customers					
	2	Accounts Payable	2010	1,200	00		
		Cash	1010			1,200	00
		Payment on account to vendors					
	3	Accounts Payable	2010	1,000	00		
		Cash	1010			1,000	00
		Rent payment due for previous month					

	4	Office Expenses & Supplies	5030	200	00			
		Cash	1010				200	00
		Interest paid to bank on long-term loan						
	5	Salaries $ Wages payable	2020	2,400	00			
		Cash	1010				2,400	00
		Paid bi-weekly salary to office manager						
	6	Unearned Revenue	2040	2,300	00			
		Sales Revenue	4010				2,300	00
		Revenue earned for books delivered to customers						
	7	Vehicle, Travelling & Entertainment Expense	5080	500	00			
		Cash	1010				500	00
		Payment of lease on truck from dealership						

Chapter 4: Elements of The Balance Sheet
Cumulative Comprehensive Hands-on Example 4

Steps in The Accounting Process					
STEP 1	**STEP 2**	**STEP 3**	**STEP 4**	**STEP 5**	**STEP 6**
Analyze Transactions	Record Journal Entries	Post to General Ledger	Prepare Trial Balance	End-of Period Adj. Entries	Compile Financial Statements

This comprehensive example covers (A) journal entries to record transactions and (B) posting of the journal entries to the related general ledger accounts of MZ LLC. See also the revised TB which follows the general ledger accounts.

Transactions:

- January 6, sold 150 books @ $60.00 each for a total of $9,000.00 on 30—day terms to customer A. Customer A promises to pay MZ LLC in 30 days.

- January 8, purchased 25 books @ $12.00 each from BooksRU2 Supplies for $300.00 payable in 30 days for Inventory.

- January 11, paid telephone bill for $175.00 on check #007

- January 13, paid office manager, salary of $800.00 for week ending January 14, 2017, on check #008.

- January 16, purchased 25 books @ $9.00 each from BooksRU2 Supplies for Inventory for $225.00 cash on check #009.

- January 18, purchased office supplies for $85.00 on check #010.

- January 21, purchased 50 books @ $8.00 each from BooksRU2 Supplies for $400.00 on 30—day terms.

- January 23, sold 50 books @ $60.00 each for a total of $3,000.00 cash to walk-in customers.

- January 24, borrowed $15,000.00 on a long-term note from the bank and purchases new packing and sorting machine for the warehouse (paid directly to machine dealer).

- January 27, paid office manager, salary of $1,600.00 for bi-weekly salary w/e Jan.28, 2017, on check #011.

- January 30, received a check for $6,000.00 advance payment from customer B for 100 books to be delivered in February.

- January 30, paid for lease on vehicle to dealership for $560.00 on check #012

Solutions to Cumulative Hands-On Example 4

(A). Journal Entries to record transactions.

Date 2017		Description	GL Ref.	Debit	Credit
General Journal			**Page No. 2**		
January	6	Accounts Receivable	1020	9,000.00	
		Sales Revenue	4010		9,000.00
		Sale 150 books to Cust. A 30-day terms			
January	8	Merchandise Inventory	1030	300.00	
		Accounts Payable	2010		300.00
		Purch. 25 books Shana's on account			
January	11	Utilities Expenses	5040	175.00	
		Cash	1010		175.00
		Telephone bill paid on check #007			
January	13	Salaries & Wages	5020	800.00	
		Cash	1010		800.00
		Office manager's salary W/E 1/14 Chk #008			
January	16	Merchandise Inventory	1030	225.00	
		Cash	1010		225.00
		Purch. 25 books Shana's chk #009			
January	18	Office Expense & Supplies	5030	85.00	
		Cash	1010		85.00
		Office supplies chk #010			
January	21	Merchandise Inventory	1030	400.00	
		Accounts Payable	2010		400.00
		Purch. 50 books Shana's 30—day term			
January	23	Cash	1010	3,000.00	
		Sales Revenue	4010		3,000.00
		Cash Sales of 50 books misc. customers			
January	24	Fixed Assets machinery	1050	15,000.00	
		Long-Term Payable	2030		15,000.00
		Bank loan and purchase of machinery			

Chapter 4: Elements of The Balance Sheet

January	27	Salaries & Wages	5020	1,600.00	
		Cash	1010		1,600.00
		Office manager's salary W/E 1/28 Chk #011			
January	30	Cash	1010	6,000.00	
		Unearned Revenue	2040		6,000.00
		Adv. Pmt from Cust. B for 100 books			
January	30	Vehicle, Travelling and Entertainment	5080	560.00	
		Cash	1010		560.00
		Automobile lease payment chk #012			

(B). Posting the Journal entries to the General Ledger accounts

General Ledger							
Account Name: Cash						Account No.: 1010	
				Post JL here		Updated Balance	
Date 2017		Trans. Description	JL Ref.	Debit	Credit	Debit	Credit
Jan.	8	Balance brought forward				12,900.00	
Jan.	11	General Journal	J2		175.00	12,725.00	
Jan.	13	General Journal	J2		800.00	11,925.00	
Jan.	16	General Journal	J2		225.00	11,700.00	
Jan.	18	General Journal	J2		85.00	11,615.00	
Jan.	23	General Journal	J2	3,000.00		14,615.00	
Jan.	27	General Journal	J2		1,600.00	13,015.00	
Jan.	30	General Journal	J2	6,000.00		19,015.00	
Jan.	30	General Journal	J2		560.00	18,455.00	

General Ledger							
Account Name: Accounts Receivable						Account No.: 1020	
				Post JL here		Updated Balance	
Date 2017		Trans. Description	JL Ref.	Debit	Credit	Debit	Credit
Jan.	6	General Journal	J2	9,000.00		9,000.00	

General Ledger

				Post JL here		Updated Balance	
Account Name: Merchandise Inventory						**Account No.:** 1030	
Date 2017		**Trans. Description**	**JL Ref.**	**Debit**	**Credit**	**Debit**	**Credit**
Jan.	6	Balance brought forward				2,000.00	
	8	General Journal	J2	300.00		2,300.00	
	16	General Journal	J2	225.00		2,525.00	
	21	General Journal	J2	400.00		2,925.00	

General Ledger

				Post JL here		Updated Balance	
Account Name: Fixed Assets						**Account No.:** 1050	
Date 2017		**Trans. Description**	**JL Ref.**	**Debit**	**Credit**	**Debit**	**Credit**
Jan.	8	Balance brought forward				2,000.00	
	24	General Journal	J2	15,000.00		17,000.00	

General Ledger

				Post JL here		Updated Balance	
Account Name: Accounts Payable						**Account No.:** 2010	
Date 2017		**Trans. Description**	**JL Ref.**	**Debit**	**Credit**	**Debit**	**Credit**
Jan.	8	General Journal	J2		300.00		300.00
	21	General Journal	J2		400.00		700.00

General Ledger

				Post JL here		Updated Balance	
Account Name: Long-Term Payable						**Account No.:** 2030	
Date 2017		**Trans. Description**	**JL Ref.**	**Debit**	**Credit**	**Debit**	**Credit**
Jan.	24	General Journal	J2		15,000.00		15,000.00

General Ledger

				Post JL here		Updated Balance	
Account Name: Unearned Revenue						**Account No.:** 2040	
Date 2017		**Trans. Description**	**JL Ref.**	**Debit**	**Credit**	**Debit**	**Credit**
Jan.	30	General Journal	J2		6,000.00		6,000.00

Chapter 4: Elements of The Balance Sheet

General Ledger

Account Name: Sales Revenue   **Account No.: 4010**

Date 2017		Trans. Description	JL Ref.	Post JL here Debit	Post JL here Credit	Updated Balance Debit	Updated Balance Credit
Jan.	6	General Journal	J2		9,000.00		9,000.00
	23	General Journal	J2		3,000.00		12,000.00

General Ledger

Account Name: Salaries & Wages   **Account No.: 5020**

Date 2017		Trans. Description	JL Ref.	Post JL here Debit	Post JL here Credit	Updated Balance Debit	Updated Balance Credit
Jan.	7	Balance Brought forward				800.00	
Jan.	13	General Journal	J2	800.00		1,600.00	
Jan.	27	General Journal	J2	1,600.00		3,200.00	

General Ledger

Account Name: Office Expense & Supplies   **Account No.: 5030**

Date 2017		Trans. Description	JL Ref.	Post JL here Debit	Post JL here Credit	Updated Balance Debit	Updated Balance Credit
Jan.	18	General Journal	J2	85.00		85.00	

General Ledger

Account Name: Utilities Expenses   **Account No.: 5040**

Date 2017		Trans. Description	JL Ref.	Post JL here Debit	Post JL here Credit	Updated Balance Debit	Updated Balance Credit
Jan.	11	General Journal	J2	175.00		175.00	

General Ledger

Account Name: Vehicle, Travelling and Entertainment   **Account No.: 5080**

Date 2017		Trans. Description	JL Ref.	Post JL here Debit	Post JL here Credit	Updated Balance Debit	Updated Balance Credit
Jan.	30	General Journal	J2	560.00		560.00	

A Simple Combined Chart of Accounts and Trial Balance, MZ LLC 01/31/2017

CHART OF ACCOUNTS	TRIAL BALANCE	
Account #, Classification, and General Ledger Descriptions	Debit $$	Credit $$

Balance Sheet

Assets: 1000

	Debit $$	Credit $$
• 1010 Cash	18,455.00	
• 1020 Accounts Receivable	9,000.00	
• 1021 Allowance for Bad Debts		XXXX.XX
• 1030 Merchandise Inventory	2,925.00	
• 1040 Prepaid Accounts	XXXX.XX	
• 1050 Fixed Assets	17,000.00	
• 1051 Accumulated Depreciation		XXXX.XX

Liabilities: 2000

	Debit $$	Credit $$
• 2010 Accounts Payable		700.00
• 2020 Salaries & Wage Payable		XXXX.XX
• 2030 Long-term Payable		15,000.00
• 2040 Unearned Revenue		6,000.00

Equity: 3000

	Debit $$	Credit $$
• 3010 Owner's Capital/Equity		20,000.00
• 3020 Drawing	XXXX.XX	
• 3030 Retained Earnings		XXXX.XX

Income Statement

Revenue: 4000

	Debit $$	Credit $$
• 4010 Sales Revenue		12,000.00
• 4020 Other Revenue		XXXX.XX
• 4030 Cost of Goods Sold (COGS)	XXXX.XX	

Expenses: 5000

	Debit $$	Credit $$
• 5010 Rent Expense	1,500.00	
• 5020 Salaries & Wages	3,200.00	
• 5030 Office Expenses & Supplies	85.00	
• 5040 Utilities Expense	175.00	
• 5050 Insurance Expense	200.00	
• 5060 Advertising & Promotion Expense	600.00	
• 5070 Depreciation Expense	XXXX.XX	
• 5080 Vehicle, Travelling & Entertainment Expense	560.00	
	XXXX.XX	
• 5090 Bad Debt Expense		
	$53,700.00	**$53,700.00**

Right margin labels: BALANCE SHEET, INCOME STATEMENT

Chapter 5: Elements of the Income Statement

Steps in The Accounting Process					
STEP 1	STEP 2	STEP 3	STEP 4	STEP 5	STEP 6
Analyze Transactions	Record Journal Entries	Post to General Ledger	Prepare Trial Balance	End-of Period Adj. Entries	Compile Financial Statements

The Income Statement AKA the Profit and Loss Statement

Important Summary of Relationship Between Revenues, Expenses, and Net Profit
If *Expenses* (including Cost of Goods Sold) are Greater than Revenues = Net *Loss* for Period
If *Revenues* are Greater than Expenses (including Cost of Goods Sold) = Net *Income* for Period

Question: What is the purpose of this chapter?

Answer: To identify the accounts in the chart of accounts used in the income statement.

The income statement, also known as the profit and loss statement, summarizes the operating activities of the organization over a period called the operating cycle of the organization. In defining the chart of accounts (COA) in chapter 2, general ledger accounts that make up the income statement were described as temporary or nominal accounts because their balances are zeroed out at the end of an operating cycle (or financial period). These accounts begin each financial period with zero balances to account for activities in the new operating cycle.

> Important Note: The **Recognition concept** in accounting is that **revenue** is recognized when **earned;** that is, when the firm has completed its obligation in the transaction. On the other hand, **expenses** are recognized immediately when **incurred** (by the firm) and is related to the **Principle of Conservatism**.

A review of the *Simple Combined Chart of Accounts and Trial Balance* at the end of previous chapters and in Appendix A, shows the categories, descriptions, and account numbers that make up the *elements* of the income statement. The chart of accounts (COA) shows the following subcategories for the income statement: Revenue account numbers beginning with the number 4; and Expense account numbers beginning with the number 5. The original transactions in previous *cumulative comprehensive hands-on examples* at the end of chapter 3 and chapter 4 should be reviewed, as they apply to the concepts and information in this chapter.

The following are descriptions, journal entries, and general ledger account balances reported on the income statement for the period ending January 31, 2017.

Revenue

Sales Revenue: 4010

Sales revenue is the life-blood of for-profit firms and the *main* source of funds used for generating income and sustaining business operations toward the goals of the firm. Revenue, or sales revenue, is derived from the sale of merchandise or services to customers who purchase the firm's products or services. Organizations sell goods or services for more than it pays to acquire the goods or provide the service, to make enough income to cover the expenses of operating the business and turn a profit. MZ LLC, our fictitious firm, sells books (merchandise inventory) to earn enough revenue to cover all expenses of the business and make a net income. Thus, the income earned from the selling of books is the *main* revenue source—sales revenue for MZ LLC.

	General Journal			Page No. 2	
Date 2017	**Description**	**GL Ref.**	**Debit**	**Credit**
Jan.	6	Accounts Receivable	1020	9,000.00	
		Sales Revenue	4010		9,000.00
		Sale 150 books to Cust. A 30-day terms			
Jan.	23	Cash	1010	3,000.00	
		Sales Revenue	4010		3,000.00
		Cash Sales of 50 books misc. customers			

General Ledger							
Account Name: Sales Revenue					**Account No.: 4010**		
				Post JL here		**Updated Balance**	
Date 2017		**Trans. Description**	**JL Ref.**	**Debit**	**Credit**	**Debit**	**Credit**
Jan.	6	General Journal	J2		9,000.00		9,000.00
	23	General Journal	J2		3,000.00		12,000.00

Other Revenue

An organization might occasionally sell non-inventoried items such as depreciated vehicles or old office equipment. These are not considered sale of merchandise and would be shown as *other revenue* on the income statement because they are not the regular main source of income for the firm.

Chapter 5: Elements of the Income Statement
Cost of Goods Sold (COGS): 4030

Cost of goods sold are the amounts paid by MZ LLC to *purchase* the books from suppliers (vendors) that were sold to customers during the period. Because the FIFO cost technique is used by the firm, we look at the FIFO table in chapter 4 to determine the cost of the 200 books sold for the month. This is an example of the matching principle in accounting, whereby revenue earned by the firm is matched with the associated costs to acquire the items sold; what the firm paid to suppliers for the items it then sold to its customers, *buying low* (at cost) and *selling high* (at sales price to customers). The 200 units were from books purchased by the firm on January 1, 2017, at $10.00 each at a total cost of $2,000.00. We therefore removed (expensed) $2,000.00 from our merchandise inventory account and recorded the expense to Cost of Goods Sold account by journal dated January 31, 2017 by debiting the Cost of Goods Sold account (A/C #4030) and crediting the Merchandise Inventory account (A/C#1030) See *adjusting entries J3* in chapter 6.

General Journal				Page No. 3	
Date 2017		**Description**	**GL Ref.**	**Debit**	**Credit**
Jan.	31	Cost of Goods Sold (COGS)	4030	2,000.00	
		Merchandise Inventory	1030		2,000.00
		COS for month under FIFO			

General Ledger							
Account Name: Cost of Goods Sold (COGS)				**Account No.: 4030**			
				Post JL here		**Updated Balance**	
Date 2017		**Trans. Description**	**JL Ref.**	**Debit**	**Credit**	**Debit**	**Credit**
Jan.	31	General Journal	J3	2,000.00		2,000.00	

Expenses

Expenses are resources used up or paid by the organization in the running of the company toward earning income and to keep the organization going. COGS are considered a special type of expense. A review of the Combined Chart of Accounts and Trial Balance on January 31, 2017, of MZ LLC at the end of chapter 4 shows the elements (G/L accounts) in the income statement of the organization and related amounts to date. Most of the titles in this section are self-explanatory.

- **Rent Expenses: 5010**

The rent expense account is used to keep track of rental expenses incurred by the organization for use of building facilities owned by third parties, such as landlord or property renting agency, usually for monthly periods. The amounts paid or due for the period (accrued) to the landlord or agency at the balance sheet date are journalized by debiting Rent Expense account and crediting the Cash account (if paid) or crediting Accounts Payable account (for unpaid rent). Only journal entries and related expense ledgers related to the sections in the chapter are shown in the tables below because we are discussing elements of the Income Statement.

General Journal				Page No. 1	
Date 2017		Description	GL Ref.	Debit	Credit
Jan	1	Rent Expense	5010	1,500.00	
		Cash	1010		1,500.00
		Chk #002 Hoggspace Inc. Whse. rent Jan.			

General Ledger							
Account Name: Rent Expense					Account No.: 5010		
				Post JL here		Updated Balance	
Date 2017		Trans. Description	JL Ref.	Debit	Credit	Debit	Credit
Jan.	1	General Journal	J1	1,500.00		1,500.00	

- **Salaries & Wages: 5020**

This account is used to keep track of amounts incurred by the firm for services provided by employees of the organization, including amounts paid or due (until next paycheck), at the balance sheet date. Only the gross amounts are shown in these examples.

General Journal				Page No. 1	
Date 2017		Description	GL Ref.	Debit	Credit
Jan	6	Salaries & Wages	5020	800.00	
		Cash	1010		800.00
		Chk #006 Office manager salary W/E Jan.07			

General Journal				Page No. 2	
Date 2017		Description	GL Ref.	Debit	Credit
Jan.	13	Salaries & Wages	5020	800.00	
		Cash	1010		800.00
		Office manager salary W/E 1/14 Chk #008			

Jan.	27	Salaries & Wages	5020	1,600.00	
		Cash	1010		1,600.00
		Office manager salary W/E 1/28 Chk #011			

General Ledger							
Account Name: Salaries & Wages						Account No.: 5020	
				Post JL here		Updated Balance	
Date 2017		Trans. Description	JL Ref.	Debit	Credit	Debit	Credit
Jan.	7	Balance Brought forward				800.00	
Jan.	13	General Journal	J2	800.00		1,600.00	
Jan.	27	General Journal	J2	1,600		3,200	
Jan.	31	General Journal	J2	320.00		3,520.00	

Employees and Independent Contractors

Organizations must distinguish between amounts paid for the services of *employees* of the firm and amounts paid for services provided by *outside* individuals and firms, called *independent contractors*. Briefly, the activities of employees are controlled directly by the human resources guidelines and policies of the firm. Independent contractors are not controlled by the firm and are expected to use their own expertise, judgement, and methods to perform services to the organization.

The distinction is important because firms are accountable to the Internal Revenue Service (IRS) for additional federal employer's payroll expenses by having employees and withhold statutory deductions from their paychecks on behalf of federal, state, and local governments. Payments to employees are recorded in the salaries and wages expense accounts.

Firms are not required to withhold statutory amounts from checks paid to independent contractors and these payments are generally recorded in the office expenses or miscellaneous expenses accounts. An IRS form 1099 is required to be sent to the independent contractor and to the Internal Revenue Service (IRS) showing the amounts paid for the year.

- **Office Expenses & Supplies: 5030**

This expense account is used to record amounts paid for small everyday office supplies such as paper and ink toner for printers, paper clips and file folders, pens and pencils used in the office etc. Office supplies are usually expensed immediately when purchased. Some organizations might use a separate asset account for Office Supplies and transfer amounts to Office Expense periodically to record amounts used up during the period. These are not mixed with regular Merchandise Inventory available for sale to customers. The journal entries to record Office Expenses and Supplies when purchased for cash are as follows:

General Journal			Page No. 2		
Date 2017		Description	GL Ref.	Debit	Credit
Jan.	18	Office Expense & Supplies	5030	85.00	
		Cash	1010		85.00
		Office supplies chk #010			

General Ledger								
Account Name: Office Expense & Supplies					Account No.: 5030			
Date 2017		Trans. Description	JL Ref.	Post JL here		Updated Balance		
				Debit	Credit	Debit	Credit	
Jan.	18	General Journal	J2	85.00		85.00		

- **Utilities Expense: 5040**

Monthly payments to telephone service companies for office telephone and fax services are charged to this account. Mobile phones used strictly for business purposes by office managers and senior executives may also be charged to this account.

General Journal			Page No. 2		
Date 2017		Description	GL Ref.	Debit	Credit
Jan.	11	Utilities Expenses	5040	175.00	
		Cash	1010		175.00
		Telephone bill paid on check #007			

General Ledger								
Account Name: Utilities Expenses					Account No.: 5040			
Date 2017		Trans. Description	JL Ref.	Post JL here		Updated Balance		
				Debit	Credit	Debit	Credit	
Jan.	11	General Journal	J2	175.00		175.00		

- **Insurance Expense: 5050**

Premiums for insurance policies on business property and liability insurance against damage to private individuals and other organizations are recorded in this account. Premiums paid on life insurance policies on the lives of senior executives are also usually recorded to this account, although a separate account may be created for this. Workers' compensation insurance payments are usually recorded in a separate Workers' Compensation Insurance Expense account.

General Journal				Page No. 1	
Date 2017		Description	GL Ref.	Debit	Credit
Jan	5	Insurance Expense	5050	200.00	
		Cash	1010		200.00
		Chk #005 Firm Status Ins. Ins. prem Jan			

General Ledger							
Account Name: Insurance Expense					Account No.: 5050		
				Post JL here		Updated Balance	
Date 2017		Trans. Description	JL Ref.	Debit	Credit	Debit	Credit
Jan.	5	General Journal	J1	200.00		200.00	

- ## Advertising & Promotion Expense: 5060

Amounts paid or due to advertising agencies for advertising or promoting the firm and its products in newspapers and electronic media, including social media, are recorded in this account.

General Journal				Page No. 1	
Date 2017		Description	GL Ref.	Debit	Credit
Jan	2	Advertising & Promotion	5060	600.00	
		Cash	1010		600.00
		Chk #003 SocMed Adverts Jan. advertising			

General Ledger							
Account Name: Advertising & Promotion					Account No.: 5060		
				Post JL here		Updated Balance	
Date 2017		Trans. Description	JL Ref.	Debit	Credit	Debit	Credit
Jan.	2	General Journal	J1	600.00		600.00	

- ## Depreciation Expense: 5070

The recorded, historical value, of fixed assets is reduced systematically over time by a process called depreciation and charged to the depreciation expense account. Depreciation is essentially the systematic spreading of the historical cost of the firm's fixed assets over current and future operating periods, matching the cost of fixed assets with periodic revenues earned while the assets are in service. It is important to recognize that assets are combined with other resources, including the expertise of employees, toward the profitable goals of an organization. As explained in chapter 4 in describing *Fixed Assets*, the depreciation concept also includes deterioration of fixed assets over time due to deteriorating operating efficiency of equipment, machines, buildings or vehicles; or items such as computer software and equipment becoming outdated or obsolete because of the introduction of new, more efficient technology.

Depreciation expense is based on estimates of the useful productive life (time) or usage (production) of an asset over which it contributes toward the earning of income for the firm (an example of the matching principle mentioned earlier for COGs). The amount calculated is recorded in the journal by debiting the depreciation expense account and crediting the related accumulated depreciation account for the period using the accumulation method.

General Journal				Page No. 3	
Date 2017		Description	GL Ref.	Debit	Credit
Jan.	31	Depreciation Expense	5070	33.33	
		Accumulated Depreciation	1051		33.33
		Month's depreciation office furniture			

General Ledger							
Account Name: Depreciation Expense						Account No.: 5070	
Date 2017		Trans. Description	JL Ref.	Post JL here		Updated Balance	
				Debit	Credit	Debit	Credit
Jan.	31	General Journal	J3	33.33		33.33	

- **Vehicle Travelling & Entertainment Expense: 5080**

Amounts posted to this account would include lease payments for company vehicles, gas, and tolls paid by the firm; travelling expenses paid for business trips such as airline, ship and train tickets; and business meals and entertainment expenses allowable by the IRS.

General Journal				Page No. 2	
Date 2017		Description	GL Ref.	Debit	Credit
Jan.	30	Vehicle, Travelling and Entertainment	5080	560.00	
		Cash	1010		560.00
		Automobile lease payment chk #012			

General Ledger							
Account Name: Vehicle, Travelling and Entertainment						**Account No.: 5080**	
				Post JL here		Updated Balance	
Date 2017		**Trans. Description**	**JL Ref.**	**Debit**	**Credit**	**Debit**	**Credit**
Jan.	30	General Journal	J2	560.00		560.00	

- **Bad Debt Expenses: 5090**

Sales to customers on terms—also called credit sales, are a major source of revenue for many organizations. These sales are usually on 30-day terms, meaning that the customer has 30 days in which to pay for goods sold and delivered to them. Credit sales are recorded in the Accounts Receivable general ledger account. Over time, some of these customers run into financial difficulties and are unable to pay amounts when they become due. Accountants estimate that a percentage of the accounts receivable balance or a percentage of the monthly sales on credit will not eventually be paid by customers and records an estimated amount to the bad debt expense account each period. See also the related definition of the *Allowance for Bad Debts* in chapter 4.

General Journal					Page No. 3	
Date 2017		**Description**	**GL Ref.**	**Debit**	**Credit**
Jan.	31	Bad Debt Expense	5090	450.00	
		Allowance for Bad Debts	1021		450.00
		Est. 5% of credit sales of $9,000.00			

General Ledger							
Account Name: Bad Debt Expense						**Account No.: 5090**	
				Post JL here		Updated Balance	
Date 2017		**Trans. Description**	**JL Ref.**	**Debit**	**Credit**	**Debit**	**Credit**
Jan.	31	General Journal	J3	450.00		450.00	

Summary

An overview of the basic structure of an accounting system and general classification, subsections, and elements (accounts) of a typical income statement was covered in this chapter. Some popular general ledger accounts found in a typical income statement were briefly described to provide understanding of how they are used in the business environment by organizations.

In the discussion of the salary and wages expense category of the income statement, a brief introduction of the characteristics and importance of distinguishing between employees and independent contractors who provide services to the organization was included.

Summary questions of financial activities chapter 5

1) Using the Chart of Accounts (COA), indicate in which general ledger account number (GL#); and financial statement, balance sheet (BS) or income statement (IS), you would find the following transactions (account DR and financial statement, then account CR and financial statement):

   a) Delivered books to prepaid customers and recognized the revenue now earned.

   b) Record the reduction in inventory for the cost of books sold during the period.

   c) Record rent (expense) due for the current period out of a prepaid rent balance.

   d) Record depreciation expenses on equipment for the period using accumulation method.

   e) Record estimate for bad debts in accounts receivable based on the allowance method.

   f) Record salary expense for current period to be paid in next period's payroll.

   g) Payment of salaries and wages earned in previous period.

Practice Journalizing Transactions 5

Reminder of steps: Each transaction would be recorded on three separate lines: (a) Debit entry, followed by (b) Credit entry, then (c) Explanation for the transaction.

1. Shipped $600.00 books to prepaid customers cash recorded in prior periods.
2. Made adjustment to inventory for cost of books sold during period for $700.00.
3. Recorded $1,000.00 rent for period out of the prepaid rent account balance.
4. Recorded $200.00 for depreciation on fixed assets using allowance method.
5. Recorded an estimated allowance of $600.00 for potential bad accounts receivable.
6. Paid salaries and wages including $3,000.00 expensed in previous period.
7. Expensed $700.00 current month's insurance premium out of prepaid account balance.

Practice Journalizing Transactions using the chart of accounts

1. GL account _____ is DR and GL account _____ is CR for $
2. GL account _____ is DR and GL account _____ is CR for $
3. GL account _____ is DR and GL account _____ is CR for $
4. GL account _____ is DR and GL account _____ is CR for $
5. GL account _____ is DR and GL account _____ is CR for $
6. GL account _____ is DR and GL account _____ is CR for $
7. GL account _____ is DR and GL account _____ is CR for $

Chapter 5: Elements of the Income Statement

Answers to Summary questions of financial activities chapter 5

1) Using the Chart of Accounts (COA), indicate in which general ledger account number (GL#); and financial statement, balance sheet (BS) or income statement (IS), you would find the following transactions (account DR and financial statement, then account CR and financial statement):

a) Shipped pre-ordered books to prepaid customers: GL# 2040 (BS), GL#4010 (IS).

b) Reduction in inventory for the cost of books sold: GL# 4030 (IS), GL#1030 (BS).

c) Record rent for the current period out of prepaid rent: GL# 5010 (IS), GL#1040 (BS).

d) Record depreciation using accumulation method: GL# 5070 (IS), GL#1051 (BS).

e) Estimate bad debts using allowance method: GL# 5090 (IS), GL#1021 (BS).

f) Record (accrue) salary expense to be paid next period: GL# 5020 (IS), GL#2020 (BS).

g) Payment of salaries and wages accrued in prior period: GL# 2020 (BS), GL#1010 (BS).

Solutions to Practice Journalizing Transactions using the chart of accounts

1. GL account 2040 is DR and GL account 4010 is CR for $600.00

2. GL account 4030 is DR and GL account 1030 is CR for $700.00

3. GL account 5010 is DR and GL account 1040 is CR for $1,000.00

4. GL account 5070 is DR and GL account 1051 is CR for $200.00

5. GL account 5090 is DR and GL account 1021 is CR for $600.00

6. GL account 2020 is DR and GL account 1010 is CR for $3,000.00

7. GL account 5050 is DR and GL account 1040 is CR for $700.00

General Journal

General Journal				Debit		Credit		Page No. 1
Date 20xx		Description	GL Ref.	Amount		Amount		
	1	Unearned Revenue	2040	600	00			
		Sales Revenue	4010			600	00	
		Shipped books to prepaid customer						
	2	Cost of Goods Sold (COGS)	4030	700	00			
		Merchandise Inventory	1030			700	00	
		Record cost of books sold for period						
	3	Rent Expenses	5010	1,000	00			
		Prepaid Accounts	1040			1,000	00	
		Rent expenses for period from prepaid rent amount						

	4	Depreciation Expense	5070	200	00		
		Accumulated Depreciation	1051			200	00
		Record depreciation on equipment					
	5	Bad Debt Expense	5090	600	00		
		Allowance for Bad Debts	1021			600	00
		Estimated doubtful accounts in AR					
	6	Salaries & Wages Payable	2020	3,000	00		
		Cash	1010			3,000	00
		Check paid for salaries and wages for prior month					
	7	Insurance Expense	5050	700	00		
		Prepaid Accounts	1040			700	00
		Insurance premium due current period					

Chapter 6: Adjusting Entries, Post-Adj. TB, Closing Entries, and Net Income

Steps in The Accounting Process					
STEP 1	**STEP 2**	**STEP 3**	**STEP 4**	**STEP 5**	**STEP 6**
Analyze Transactions	Record Journal Entries	Post to General Ledger	Prepare Trial Balance	End-of Period Adj. Entries	Compile Financial Statements

Question: What is the purpose of this chapter?

Answer: To determine the net profit or loss for the period, by summarizing and closing out the balances in the temporary accounts in the income statement.

Adjusting Entries

At the end of an operating, accountants make adjusting journal entries for unrecorded revenue and expenses to determine the *true* operating results for the period. This is necessary because payment for some resources used by the firm might not have been made or paid in advance, or transfers from unearned revenues to recognize actual revenues earned, might need to be recorded to determine the true profit or loss for the period. Examples of such adjustments include: payments made in advance for insurance and rent, called prepaid expense (technically prepaid assets); accruals for unpaid wages and salaries of employees; depreciation expense, estimate for bad debts; interest accrued on long-term debts; reclass from unearned revenue to revenue; and inventory adjustments and cost of sales.

The following adjusting entries were made on January 31, 2017, for MZ LLC, and the resulting effects on the general ledger accounts shown below the entries.

- Jan. 31 Estimated 5% of sales on *terms* for the month will eventually not be paid and recorded the appropriate allowance for bad debts. Recorded $450.00 ($9,000.00 x 0.05) to bad debt expense.

- Jan. 31 Recorded accrued Wages and Salaries payable of $320.00 (2/5 x $800.00) for period ending January 31 which will be included in the next bi-weekly paycheck.

- Jan. 31 Estimated and recorded one month's straight-line depreciation expense on office desks and chairs purchased on January 1, depreciable over 5 years (60 months) with no residual value. 1/60 x $2,000.00 = $33.33.

- Adjust Merchandise Inventory to Cost of Sales amounting to $2,000.00 for merchandise sold during month using FIFO (see FIFO table earlier in chapter), using the *periodic* inventory adjustment method, whereby the balance in the inventory account is adjusted at the end of an operating period instead of *perpetually* after each transaction.

Adjusting General Journal					Page No. 3
Date 2017		Description	GL Ref.	Debit	Credit
Jan.	31	Cost of Goods Sold (COGS)	4030	2,000.00	
		Merchandise Inventory	1030		2,000.00
		COS for month under FIFO			
Jan.	31	Salaries & Wages Expense	5020	320.00	
		Salaries & Wages Payable	2020		320.00
		2 days wages accrued for office manager.			
Jan.	31	Depreciation Expense	5070	33.33	
		Accumulated Depreciation	1051		33.33
		Month's depreciation office furniture			
Jan.	31	Bad Debt Expense	5090	450.00	
		Allowance for Bad Debts	1021		450.00
		Est. 5% of credit sales of $9,000.00			

Adjustments for Cost of Goods Sold

General Ledger							
Account Name: Cost of Goods Sold (COGS)						Account No.: 4030	
				Post JL here		Updated Balance	
Date 2017		Trans. Description	JL Ref.	Debit	Credit	Debit	Credit
Jan.	31	General Journal	J3	2,000.00		2,000.00	

General Ledger							
Account Name: Merchandise Inventory						Account No.: 1030	
				Post JL here		Updated Balance	
Date 2017		Trans. Description	JL Ref.	Debit	Credit	Debit	Credit
Jan.	6	Balance brought forward				2,000.00	
Jan.	8	General Journal	J2	300.00		2,300.00	
Jan.	16	General Journal	J2	225.00		2,525.00	
Jan.	21	General Journal	J2	400.00		2,925.00	
Jan.	31	General journal	J3		2,000.00	925.00	

Adjustments for Accrual of Unpaid Salaries and Wages: 5020

General Ledger							
Account Name: Salaries & Wages					**Account No.: 5020**		
				Post JL here		Updated Balance	
Date 2017		Trans. Description	JL Ref.	Debit	Credit	Debit	Credit
Jan.	7	Balance Brought forward				800.00	
Jan.	13	General Journal	J2	800.00		1,600.00	
Jan.	27	General Journal	J2	1,600.00		3,200.00	
Jan.	31	General Journal	J3	320.00		3,520.00	

General Ledger							
Account Name: Salaries & Wages Payable					**Account No.: 2020**		
				Post JL here		Updated Balance	
Date 2017		Trans. Description	JL Ref.	Debit	Credit	Debit	Credit
Jan.	31	General Journal	J3		320.00		320.00

Adjustments for Estimated Depreciation

General Ledger							
Account Name: Depreciation Expense					**Account No.: 5070**		
				Post JL here		Updated Balance	
Date 2017		Trans. Description	JL Ref.	Debit	Credit	Debit	Credit
Jan.	31	General Journal	J3	33.33		33.33	

General Ledger							
Account Name: Accumulated Depreciation					**Account No.: 1051**		
				Post JL here		Updated Balance	
Date 2017		Trans. Description	JL Ref.	Debit	Credit	Debit	Credit
Jan.	31	General Journal	J3		33.33		33.33

Adjustments for Estimated Bad Debts

General Ledger							
Account Name: Bad Debt Expense					**Account No.: 5090**		
				Post JL here		Updated Balance	
Date 2017		Trans. Description	JL Ref.	Debit	Credit	Debit	Credit
Jan.	31	General Journal	J3	450.00		450.00	

General Ledger							
Account Name: Allowance for Bad Debts					Account No.: 1021		
				Post JL here		Updated Balance	
Date 2017		Trans. Description	JL Ref.	Debit	Credit	Debit	Credit
Jan.	31	General Journal	J3		450.00		450.00

After the adjusting entries are completed and posted to the general ledger accounts, a *post-adjustment* trial balance is prepared, and the debit and credit columns totaled to check that they are equal in accordance with the double-entry accounting concept discussed earlier. A review of the Post-Adjustment Chart of Accounts and Trial Balance on the next page shows the totals of the Debit and Credit columns are equal (also referred to as footing the TB). After the accountant has reviewed the TB and is satisfied that it is in order, he or she proceeds to the next phase of the systematic steps: *closing the books*.

Closing the books refers to closing out all the nominal or temporary revenue and expense accounts by transferring their balances to another temporary, transitionary account, the income summary account, which is then closed out to the retained earnings account.

New General Ledger Account: Income Summary Account

I waited until the new learner was introduced and exposed to other major types of general ledger accounts found in a typical chart of accounts (COA), especially the revenue and expense (temporary accounts), to introduce the *Income Summary* general ledger account. This account is not a typical general ledger account and is used temporarily at the end of the accounting period to close all amounts in the nominal or temporary accounts in the income statement and determine the net profit or loss for the period. The account, 3900 Income Summary, will be added to the COA as a *clearing account* for revenues and expenses, and the ending balance in this account subsequently closed out to the Retained Earnings account #3030 in the balance sheet.

Post-Adjustment Chart of Accounts and Trial Balance, MZ LLC 01/31/2017

CHART OF ACCOUNTS Account #, Classification and General Ledger Descriptions	TRIAL BALANCE Debit $$	Credit $$
Balance Sheet		
Assets: 1000		
• 1010 Cash	18,455.00	
• 1020 Accounts Receivable	9,000.00	
• 1021 Allowance for Bad Debts		450.00
• 1030 Merchandise Inventory	925.00	
• 1040 Prepaid Accounts	XXXX.XX	
• 1050 Fixed Assets	17,000.00	
• 1051 Accumulated Depreciation		33.33
Liabilities: 2000		
• 2010 Accounts Payable		700.00
• 2020 Salaries & Wage Payable		320.00
• 2030 Long-term Payable		15,000.00
• 2040 Unearned Revenue		6,000.00
Equity: 3000		
• 3010 Owner's Capital/Equity		20,000.00
• 3020 Drawing	XXXX.XX	
• 3030 Retained Earnings		XXXX.XX
Income Statement		
Revenue: 4000		
• 4010 Sales Revenue		12,000.00
• 4020 Other Revenue		XXXX.XX
• 4030 Cost of Goods Sold (COGS)	2,000.00	
Expenses: 5000		
• 5010 Rent Expense	1,500.00	
• 5020 Salaries & Wages	3,520.00	
• 5030 Office Expenses & Supplies	85.00	
• 5040 Utilities Expense	175.00	
• 5050 Insurance Expense	200.00	
• 5060 Advertising & Promotion Expense	600.00	
• 5070 Depreciation Expense	33.33	
• 5080 Vehicle, Travelling & Entertainment Expense	560.00	
• 5090 Bad Debt Expense	450.00	
	$54,503.33	$54,503.33

BALANCE SHEET

INCOME STATEMENT

The following tables show the closing entries for the nominal (temporary accounts) to the income summary account; the balances in the nominal general ledger accounts; and the income statement of MZ LLC for the period ending January 31, 2017.

End of Period Closing Entries

Closing Journal			Page No. 4		
Date 2017		Description	GL Ref.	Debit	Credit
Jan.	31	Sales Revenue	4010	12,000.00	
		Income Summary	3900		12,000.00
		Close Sales Revenue to Income Summary			
Jan.	31	Income Summary	3900	2,000.00	
		Cost of Goods Sold	4030		2,000.00
		Close COGS to Income Summary			
Jan.	31	Income Summary	3900	1,500.00	
		Rent Expense	5010		1,500.00
		Close Rent Expense to Income Summary			
Jan.	31	Income Summary	3900	3,520.00	
		Salaries & Wages Expense	5020		3,520.00
		Close Sal. & Wages to Income Summary			
Jan.	31	Income Summary	3900	85.00	
		Office Expenses & Supplies	5030		85.00
		Close Of. Expenses to Income Summary			
Jan.	31	Income Summary	3900	175.00	
		Utilities Expense	5040		175.00
		Close Sales Revenue to Income Summary			
Jan.	31	Income Summary	3900	200.00	
		Insurance Expense	5050		200.00
		Close Ins. Exps. to Income Summary			
Jan.	31	Income Summary	3900	600.00	
		Advertising & Promotion	5060		600.00
		Close Adv. & Prom. to Income Summary			

Chapter 6: Adjusting Entries, Post-Adj. TB, Closing Entries, and Net Income

Jan.	31	Income Summary	3900		33.33	
		Depreciation Expense	5070			33.33
		Close Depr. Exp. to Income Summary				
Jan.	31	Income Summary	3900		560.00	
		Vehicle, Travelling & Entertainment	5080			560.00
		Close Trav. & Ent. to Income Summary				
Jan.	31	Income Summary	3900		450.00	
		Bad Debt Expense	5090			450.00
		Close Bad Debt Exp. to Income Summary				
Jan.	31	Income Summary	3900		2,867.67	
		Retained Earnings	3030			2,876.67
		Close Income Summary to Retained Earn.				

Note: The final entry closes out a credit balance (Net Income) in the income summary account (3900) to the retained earnings account (3030).

General Ledger

Account Name: Retained Earnings   **Account No.: 3030**

Date 2017		Trans. Description	JL Ref.	Post JL here Debit	Post JL here Credit	Updated Balance Debit	Updated Balance Credit
Jan.	31	Closing Journal	J4		2,876.67		2,876.67

General Ledger

Account Name: Income Summary   **Account No.: 3900**

Date 2017		Trans. Description	JL Ref.	Post JL here Debit	Post JL here Credit	Updated Balance Debit	Updated Balance Credit
Jan.	31	Closing Journal	J4		12,000.00		12,000.00
Jan.	31	Closing Journal	J4	2,000.00			10,000.00
Jan.	31	Closing Journal	J4	1,500.00			8,500.00
Jan.	31	Closing Journal	J4	3,520.00			4,980.00
Jan.	31	Closing Journal	J4	85.00			4,895.00
Jan.	31	Closing Journal	J4	175.00			4,720.00
Jan.	31	Closing Journal	J4	200.00			4,520.00
Jan.	31	Closing Journal	J4	600.00			3,920.00
Jan.	31	Closing Journal	J4	33.33			3,886.67

Jan.	31	Closing Journal	J4	560.00			3,326.67
Jan.	31	Closing Journal	J4	450.00			2,876.67
Jan.	31	Closing Journal	J4	2,876.67			0.00

General Ledger

Account Name: Sales Revenue						Account No.: 4010	
				Post JL here		Updated Balance	
Date 2017		Trans. Description	JL Ref.	Debit	Credit	Debit	Credit
Jan.	6	General Journal	J2		9,000.00		9,000.00
	23	General Journal	J2		3,000.00		12,000.00
Jan.	31	Closing Journal	J4	12,000.00			0.00

General Ledger

Account Name: Cost of Goods Sold (COGS)						Account No.: 4030	
				Post JL here		Updated Balance	
Date 2017		Trans. Description	JL Ref.	Debit	Credit	Debit	Credit
Jan.	31	General Journal	J2	2,000.00		2,000.00	
Jan.	31	Closing Journal	J4		2,000.00	0.00	

General Ledger

Account Name: Rent Expense						Account No.: 5010	
				Post JL here		Updated Balance	
Date 2017		Trans. Description	JL Ref.	Debit	Credit	Debit	Credit
Jan.	1	General Journal	J1	1,500.00		1,500.00	
Jan.	31	Closing Journal	J4		1,500.00	0.00	

General Ledger

Account Name: Salaries & Wages						Account No.: 5020	
				Post JL here		Updated Balance	
Date 2017		Trans. Description	JL Ref.	Debit	Credit	Debit	Credit
Jan.	7	Balance Brought forward				800.00	
Jan.	13	General Journal	J2	800.00		1,600.00	
Jan.	27	General Journal	J2	1,600		3,200	
Jan.	31	General Journal	J2	320.00		3,520.00	
Jan.	31	Closing Journal	J4		3,520.00	0.00	

General Ledger

Account Name: Office Expense & Supplies						Account No.: 5030	
Date 2017		Trans. Description	JL Ref.	Post JL here		Updated Balance	
				Debit	Credit	Debit	Credit
Jan.	18	General Journal	J2	85.00		85.00	
Jan.	31	Closing Journal	J4		85.00	0.00	

General Ledger

Account Name: Utilities Expenses						Account No.: 5040	
Date 2017		Trans. Description	JL Ref.	Post JL here		Updated Balance	
				Debit	Credit	Debit	Credit
Jan.	11	General Journal	J2	175.00		175.00	
Jan.	31	Closing Journal	J4		175.00	0.00	

General Ledger

Account Name: Insurance Expense						Account No.: 5050	
Date 2017		Trans. Description	JL Ref.	Post JL here		Updated Balance	
				Debit	Credit	Debit	Credit
Jan.	5	General Journal	J1	200.00		200.00	
Jan.	31	Closing Journal	J4		200.00	0.00	

General Ledger

Account Name: Advertising & Promotion						Account No.: 5060	
Date 2017		Trans. Description	JL Ref.	Post JL here		Updated Balance	
				Debit	Credit	Debit	Credit
Jan.	2	General Journal	J1	600.00		600.00	
Jan.	31	Closing Journal	J4		600.00	0.00	

General Ledger

Account Name: Depreciation Expense						Account No.: 5070	
Date 2017		Trans. Description	JL Ref.	Post JL here		Updated Balance	
				Debit	Credit	Debit	Credit
Jan.	31	General Journal	J2	33.33		33.33	
Jan.	31	Closing Journal	J4		33.33	0.00	

General Ledger

Account Name: Vehicle, Travelling and Entertainment						Account No.: 5080	
				Post JL here		**Updated Balance**	
Date 2017		**Trans. Description**	**JL Ref.**	**Debit**	**Credit**	**Debit**	**Credit**
Jan.	30	General Journal	J2	560.00		560.00	
Jan.	31	Closing Journal	J4		560.00	0.00	

General Ledger

Account Name: Bad Debt Expense						Account No.: 5090	
				Post JL here		**Updated Balance**	
Date 2017		**Trans. Description**	**JL Ref.**	**Debit**	**Credit**	**Debit**	**Credit**
Jan.	31	General Journal	J2	450.00		450.00	
Jan.	31	Closing Journal	J4		450.00	0.00	

The Income Statement

MZ LLC. Income Statement

For Period Ended January 31, 2017

	$	$
Sales Revenue		
Sales:		12,000.00
Less Cost of Goods Sold:		(2,000.00)
Gross Profit		10,000.00
Expenses	$	$
Rent Expense	1,500.00	
Salaries & Wages	3,520.00	
Office Expenses & Supplies	85.00	
Utilities Expense	175.00	
Insurance Expense	200.00	
Advertising & Promotion Expense	600.00	
Depreciation Expense	33.33	
Vehicle, Trav. & Ent. Expenses	560.00	
Bad Debt Expenses	450.00	
Total Expenses		7,123.33
Net Income		2,876.67

Notice how the temporary (nominal) accounts are displayed in the income statement.

MZ LLC made net income of $2,876.67 during the first month of operation: The $10,000.00 Gross profit of $10,000.00 was more than the $7,123.33 Expenses.

Chapter 6: Adjusting Entries, Post-Adj. TB, Closing Entries, and Net Income

The $12,000.00 credit balance in the Sales Revenue account was greater than the combined debit balances in the expense accounts of 7,123.33 and cost of sales account of $2,000.00.

Important Summary of Relationship Between Revenues, Expenses, and Net Profit

If *Revenues* are Greater than *Expenses* (including Cost of Goods Sold) = Net Income for Period

Revenues $12,000.00 are Greater than Expenses $9,123.33 (including Cost of Goods Sold) = Net *Income* $2,876.33 for Period

Summary

In this chapter, we demonstrated the systematic steps taken by accountants to record, post, adjust, and close out the ending balances in the temporary general ledger accounts for revenue and expenses to the income summary account. We then closed the ending balance amount in the income summary account (Acct. #3900) to the retained earnings account (Acct. #3030)—a permanent account reported in the equity section of the balance sheet. The chapter ended with a preview of the income statement of MZ LLC, and how the closed temporary accounts are categorized and shown on the statement. We will discuss the main financial statements in the next chapter and show the next step in the systematic step-by-step accounting procedures to *report* the results of the operating activities for the period, and show the resources owned and owed by the firm at the end of the fiscal period.

Summary questions of financial activities chapter 6

1) Using the Chart of Accounts (COA), indicate the groups of general ledger account numbers (GL#) are used in the income statement and why.

2) Using the Chart of Accounts (COA), indicate (a) which groups of account numbers are closed out at the end of the fiscal year and why; (b) what they are called (temporary or permanent); and (c) to which account in the balance sheet are the amounts in the temporary accounts in the income statement ultimately closed at the end of the fiscal period.

Chapter 6: Adjusting Entries, Post-Adj. TB, Closing Entries, and Net Income

Answers to Summary questions of financial activities chapter 1

1) Using the Chart of Accounts (COA), indicate the groups of general ledger account numbers (GL#) are used in the income statement and why.

    Revenue account numbers—4####, and Expense account numbers—5####. They are used to determine the net profit or loss of the operating activities of the business for the period.

2) Using the Chart of Accounts (COA), indicate (a) Revenue account numbers—4####, and Expense account numbers—5#### are closed out at the end of the fiscal year to determine profit or loss for the period and to start the subsequent period with zero balances; (b) they are called temporary or nominal accounts; and (c) the ending balances in the temporary accounts are first closed out to and interim income summary account; the income summary account is then closed out to the retained earnings account, a permanent account, in the balance sheet at the end of the fiscal period.

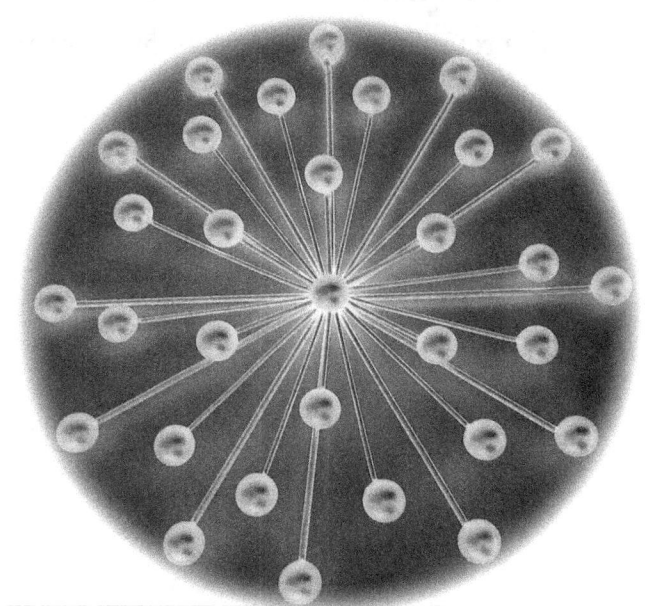

Collaborative learning. "Superior learners seek at least two to six
additional sources of information." Dr. Denver Pettigrew

Chapter 7: Income Statement, Balance Sheet, Changes in Owner's Equity

Steps in The Accounting Process					
STEP 1	**STEP 2**	**STEP 3**	**STEP 4**	**STEP 5**	**STEP 6**
Analyze Transactions	Record Journal Entries	Post to General Ledger	Prepare Trial Balance	End-of Period Adj. Entries	Compile Financial Statements

Question: What is the purpose of this chapter?

Answer: To introduce the main financial statement reports of a firm and learn the relationships between them.

We have completed the activities shown in steps 1 to 5 of the accounting process to record and post business transactions in the journal and related general ledger accounts; closed the temporary accounts and prepared the income statement; and determined and transfer net income to the retained earnings in the balance sheet, we will now look at the financial statement reports of our hypothetical business, MZ LLC, as at January 31, 2017. The income statement is shown in the following table:

The Income Statement

MZ LLC. Income Statement For Period Ended January 31, 2017		
Sales Revenue	$	$
Sales:		12,000.00
Less Cost of Goods Sold:		(2,000.00)
Gross Profit		**10,000.00**
Expenses	$	$
Rent Expense	1,500.00	
Salaries & Wages	3,520.00	
Office Expenses & Supplies	85.00	
Utilities Expense	175.00	
Insurance Expense	200.00	
Advertising & Promotion Expense	600.00	
Depreciation Expense	33.33	
Vehicle, Trav. & Ent. Expenses	560.00	
Bad Debt Expenses	450.00	
Total Expenses		**7,123.33**
Net Income		**2,876.67**

The net income for the period is transferred to the retained earnings account balance and shown in the equity section of the balance sheet, and all temporary accounts now contain zero balances in preparation for the next accounting period. This is depicted in the following diagram:

Relationship Between Income Statement and The Balance Sheet

1

Income Statement Containing Temporary Expense and Revenue Accounts

+ Expense Accounts	**And**	-Revenue Accounts
+4030+5010+5020+5030+5040+5050+5060+5070+5080+5090		-4010-4020

These temporary accounts are closed out to the Income Summary account as Net Income or Net Loss for the period

If Expenses > Revenues = Net Loss; If Expenses < Revenues = Net Income for the Period

The temporary Income Summary account is closed out to the Retained Earnings account, a Permanent account in the Balance Sheet

2

Net Income to Retained Earnings Account—Permanent Account in Balance Sheet

Net Income/Loss is added to/subtracted from the beginning amount in the Retained Earnings account, 3030, to determine the ending balance of Retained Earnings shown in the Equity section of the Balance Sheet

3

Balance Sheet –Permanent Accounts

Assets:1010+1020-1021+1030+1040+1050-1051 = **Liabilities**: 2010+2020+2030+2040 Plus **Equity**: 3010-3020+3030

The Statement of Retained Earnings

Some organizations account for changes in the balance of the retained earnings account, a permanent account reported in the balance sheet, by combining the information in the income statement, after arriving at the net income for the period. It is common, however, to prepare a separate statement of retained earnings to indicate the intermediary relationship between the income statement and the balance sheet. The structure of the statement of retained earnings is like the Statement of Changes in Owner's Equity described later in the chapter.

MZ LLC Statement of Retained Earnings Jan. 1 to Jan. 31, 2017

	$$
Retained Earnings	
Balance December 31, 2016	0.00
Add Net income or Less Net Loss from Income Statement for period	2,876.67
Balance in Retained Earnings January 31, 2017	$2,876.67

The statement of retained earnings is sometimes included with the income statement in a combined statement of income and retained earnings.

MZ LLC. Combined Income Statement & Retained Earnings
For Period Ended January 31, 2017

	$	$
Sales Revenue		
Sales:		12,000.00
Less Cost of Goods Sold:		(2,000.00)
Gross Profit		**10,000.00**
Expenses	$	$
Rent Expense	1,500.00	
Salaries & Wages	3,520.00	
Office Expenses & Supplies	85.00	
Utilities Expense	175.00	
Insurance Expense	200.00	
Advertising & Promotion Expense	600.00	
Depreciation Expense	33.33	
Vehicle, Trav. & Ent. Expenses	560.00	
Bad Debt Expenses	450.00	
Total Expenses		7,123.33
Net Income		2,876.67
Retained Earnings		
Balance December 31, 2016		0.00
Add Net income or Less Net Loss from Income Statement for period		2,876.67
Balance in Retained Earnings January 31, 2017		$2,876.67

Review the balance sheet section of the *Post-Adjustment Chart of Accounts and Trial Balance* in the previous chapter and the Combined Statement of Income & Retained Earnings shown above. We can now show the final balance of $2,876.67 from the statement of retained earnings account 3030 in the equity section of the balance sheet. The completed balance sheet report and statement of changes in owner's equity report are as shown on the next page.

The Balance Sheet

MZ LLC Balance Sheet as at Period Ending January 31, 2017

	$$	$$
Assets		
Cash		18,455.00
Accounts Receivable	9,000.00	
Less Allowance for Bad Debts	(450.00	
Net Accounts Receivable		8,550.00
Merchandise Inventory		925.00
Total Current Assets		27,930.00
Fixed Assets	17,000.00	
Less Accumulated Depreciation	(33.33)	
Net Fixed Assets		16,966.67
Total Assets (A)		$44,896.67
Liabilities		
Accounts Payable		700.00
Salaries & Wages Payable		320.00
Unearned Revenue		6,000.00
Total Current Liabilities		7,020.00
Long-term Payable		15,000.00
Total Liabilities (L)		$22,020.00
Owners' Equity		
Owners' Capital/Equity		20,000.00
Retained Earnings		2,876.67
Total Equity (E)		$22,876.67
Total Liabilities + Equity (L+E) = (A)		$44,896.67

The Statement of Changes in Owner's Equity/Stockholder's Equity

MZ LLC Statement of Changes in Owner's Equity Jan. 1 to Jan. 31, 2017

	$$
Owners' Equity	
January 1, Beginning Owners' Capital/Equity	0.00
Add Capital Contributed Master Zen	20,000.00
Loss for Period Posted to Retained Earnings	2,876.67
Less Drawings by Owners for the Period	0.00
Total Equity (E) January 31, 2017	$22,876.67

The statement of changes in owner's equity is a report showing in detail why the balance of the equity account of the organization increased, or decreased, from the beginning to the end of the current reporting period. The report shows (a) there was no balance in the account at the start of the period, January 1, 2017; (b) that Master Zen, the owner of the business, invested $20,000.00 to capitalize the organization; (c) there was no withdrawal for personal use by the owner; and (d) the organization made net operating income of $2,876.67 for the month, to arrive at the ending balance of $22,876.67 in the owner's equity account.

Summary

In this chapter, we reviewed four financial statements for MZ LLC for the period ending January 31, 2017: (1) Income Statement, (2) Statement of Retained Earnings, (3) Balance Sheet, and (4) Statement of Changes in Owner's Equity. You should study how the financial statements are interrelated: the net income or loss for the period in the income statement is closed out to the retained earnings account and reported in the owner's equity section of the balance sheet. We will explore another important financial statement, the cash flows statement, along with the bank reconciliation statement in chapter 8.

Chapter 8: The Cash Flows and Bank Reconciliation Statements

Steps in The Accounting Process					
STEP 1	**STEP 2**	**STEP 3**	**STEP 4**	**STEP 5**	**STEP 6**
Analyze Transactions	Record Journal Entries	Post to General Ledger	Prepare Trial Balance	End-of Period Adj. Entries	Compile Financial Statements

Question: What is the purpose of this chapter?

Answer: To demonstrate how direct and indirect cash flows methods and bank reconciliation statements are constructed.

Two statements that appear to provide great challenges to new learners are (1) cash flows statement, and (2) the bank reconciliation statement. The cash flows statement is sometimes called the statement of *sources and uses* of cash.

The Cash Flows Statement

The cash flows statement is a report summarizing the *changes* in the balance of the *cash account* between the start and the end of a firm's operating cycle or financial period, showing the sources and usage of cash by the firm for the period. The *change* in the cash account balance is classified as financing, investing, and operating cash flows in the statement of cash flows. In other words, the purpose of cash flows statements is to identify what caused the cash account balance to change for the period and classify the reasons. Identifying the causes is done by analyzing the non-cash accounts (assets, liabilities, and equity accounts) in the balance sheet along with items from the income statement for the period. To prepare the cash flows statements we will need to study the financial statements to find the following:

- ❖ By what amount did the cash account change between the start and end of the period? Simply deduct the beginning balance from the ending balance to identify the *change* in the cash account.
- ❖ What was the net income for the period as shown in the Income Statement?
- ❖ Use a comparative Balance Sheet to identify the non-cash accounts—all other accounts except the cash account—and calculate the changes in their balances for the period (between the start and end of the current period).

    Note: the *start* of the *current* period is also the *end* of the *previous* period.

- ❖ Summarize and classify the changes in the non-cash account into three groups, (1) Financing cash flows, which includes receipt and payments of major sources of cash for funding the business such as obtaining and repaying major bank loans and equity funding and drawings; (2) Investing cash flows, which entail purchase and disposal of long-term fixed assets; and (3) Operating cash flows are the remaining cash flows other than those in financing and investing cash flows. The operating cash flows are listed first in the cash flows statements, followed by investing cash flows, and then financing cash flows.

Operating cash flows represent the bulk of cash activities of a business because it involves the receipts and payments for the main value-creating activities for earning revenue and increasing profits for the firm. Operating cash flows are directly or indirectly related to the income statement and the current assets and liabilities of the balance sheet and include: receipts from, and sales to customers—cash and on terms (receivable); purchases from, and payments to suppliers for merchandize, services of employees, rent, insurance etc.

We will use the Comparative Balance Sheet to identify the cash and non-cash accounts and the Income Statement to prepare the cash flows statements.

INCOME STMT. & STMT OF RET. EARNINGS

MZ LLC. Combined Income Statement & Statement of Retained Earnings		
For Period Ended January 31, 2017		
Sales Revenue	$	$
Sales:		12,000.00
Less Cost of Goods Sold:		(2,000.00)
Gross Profit		**10,000.00**
Expenses	$	$
Rent Expense	1,500.00	
Salaries & Wages	3,520.00	
Office Expenses & Supplies	85.00	
Utilities Expense	175.00	
Insurance Expense	200.00	
Advertising & Promotion Expense	600.00	
Depreciation Expense	33.33	
Vehicle, Trav. & Ent. Expenses	560.00	
Bad Debt Expenses	450.00	
Total Expenses		(7,123.33)
Net Income/(Loss)		2,876.67
Add Previous Retained Earnings Balance		0.00
Less Drawings by Owner for Period		0.00
Current Y/E Retained Earnings Balance		2,876.67

COMPARATIVE BALANCE SHEET

MZ LLC Comparative Balance Sheet as at January 31, 2017

	January 31, 2017	January 31, 2017	December 31, 2016	
Assets	$$	$$	$$	
Cash		18,455.00	0.00	*Cash AC*
Accounts Receivable	9,500.00			
Less Allowance for Bad Debts	(450.00			
Net Accounts Receivable		8,550.00	0.00	
Merchandise Inventory		925.00	0.00	
Total Current Assets		27,930.00	0.00	
Fixed Assets	17,000.00			
Less Accumulated Depreciation	(33.33)			
Net Fixed Assets		16,966.67	0.00	
Total Assets (A)		$44,896.67	$0.00	
Liabilities				
Accounts Payable		700.00	0.00	
Salaries & Wages Payable		320.00	0.00	
Unearned Revenue		6,000.00	0.00	
Total Current Liabilities		7,020.00	0.00	
Long-term Payable		15,000.00	0.00	
Total Liabilities (L)		$22,020.00	$0.00	
Owners' Equity				
Owners' Capital/Equity		20,000.00	0.00	
Retained Earnings		2,876.67	0.00	
Total Equity (E)		$22,876.67	$0.00	
Total Liabilities + Equity (L+E) = (A)		$44,896.67	$0.00	

(Right margin, vertical text: NON-CASH ACCOUNTS)

The first step in preparing the cash flows statement is to identify the change in the cash account balance for the period ending January 31. The amount in MZ LLC's cash account on December 31, 2016, was zero before the owner's capital contribution of $20,000.00 on 1st January 2017, and on January 31, 2017 the balance was, $18,455.00. Therefore, the net *change* is $18,455.00.00 ($00.00 - $18,455.00) for the period. This change will be analyzed and summarized by using the non-cash accounts to identify the sources and uses into three categories: *operating*, *investing*, and *financing*. See the transactions recorded previously in the journals in chapters 2, 3 and 4.

> **Important Reminder: The Cash Flows Statement is used to analyze the _change_ in the cash account for the period and summarize the _change_ into three categories: (1) Operating, (2) Investing, and (3) Financing.**

There are two methods used for statements of cash flows: the *direct* method and the *indirect* method.

Direct method

The direct method for cash flows statements analyzes the transactions posted to the cash account ledger and categorizes them as operating, investing, or financing *directly* on the cash flows statement. Two approaches to the direct method are (a) analyzing and classifying each transaction posted in the cash account for the period; and (b) analyzing and classifying transactions posted to the *non-cash accounts* on the balance sheet and income statement for the cash components for the period. Both approaches achieve the same results: identifying the receipts and payments (sources and uses) of cash for the period and categorizes them as operating, investing, and financing *directly* on the cash flows statement.

To understand the cash flows statements, study the following diagrams:

The Direct Cash Flows Method

Direct Method: Statement of Cash Flows Cash Account 1010 for Period Ending January 31, 2017								
Bal. Jan. 1, 2017	Plus (+) or minus (-)	**Net Operating flows**	Plus (+) or minus (-)	**Net Investing flows**	Plus (+) or minus (-)	**Net Financing flows**	Bal. Jan. 31, 2017	
$0.00		$455.00		-$17,000.00		+$35,000.00	$18,455.00	
Sources—inflows (deposits) of cash (+) and Uses—outflows (payments) of cash went (-) for the period								
		Operating flows		**Investing flows**		**Financing flows**		
Details of operating, investing, and financing deposits and payments in the cash account.		Merch. -$2,225.00, Sales +$3,000.00, Sales Adv. +$6,000.0 Expenses -$6,320.00		Off. Furn. -$2,000.00, mach. -$15,000.00,		Capital/Equity from Owner +$20,000.00 plus Bank loan $15,000.00		

The Statement of Cash Flows using the direct method:

Net Operating Cash Flows		
Receipts from Sales	3,000.00	
Advance receipts from customers	6,000.00	9,000.00
Payments to suppliers	-2,225.00	
Payments to employees	-3,200.00	
Payments to telephone co.	-175.00	
Payments for office supplies	-85.00	
Payments to auto dealership	-560.00	
Payments to landlord	-1,500.00	
Payments to insurance Co.	-200.00	
Payments to advertising Co.	-600.00	-8,545.00
		455.00
Net Investing Cash Flows		
Payments for office equipment	-2000.00	
Payment for sorting machine	-15,000	**-17,000.00**
Net Financing Cash Flows		
Cash investment from owner	20,000.00	
Receipt of long-term loan from bank	15,000.00	**35,000.00**
Total Change in Cash Position		**18,455.00**

Note: In the *direct* method, the sources and uses of receipts and payments posted in the cash account for the period are identified and displayed directly in the appropriate sections of the statement as operating, investing, or financing cash flows. This can be cumbersome for firms with large amounts of cash transactions in operating the business for the period.

The Indirect Method

Instead of analyzing every transaction in each non-cash balance sheet account to identify the cash received or used in the operating section of the cash flows statement as in the direct method, the *indirect* method identifies the *changes* in the current assets and current liabilities sections of the balance sheet to determine the sources and uses of cash in the operating activities for the period. This method uses comparative balance sheets to calculate the changes in the ending balances of the non-cash the accounts in consecutive balance sheets, along with the net income or loss from the income statement and adding back depreciation expenses for the period. This is shown in the table below. Notice the totals are identical to the summarized operating, investing, and financing sections in the direct method. The indirect cash flows method is much quicker and easier to complete and is the method used by most organizations to report the sources and uses of cash for the period, especially to identify if the business operations for the period brought in more cash than was spent.

The Indirect Cash Flows Method

GL Accts	Flow Types	January 31, 2017 A		December 31, 2016 B		Period Changes A - B		Statement of Cash Flows	
	O, I, F	Debit	Credit	Debit	Credit	Debit	Credit	**Operating Activities: (O)**	
ASSETS								N. Inc./-Loss	2,876.67
1010. Cash	Not used in the indirect method as this is the account being analyzed							Add deprec.	+33.33
1020 Accounts Receivable	O	9,000.00		0.00		9,000.00		Net Current Assets	-9,475.00
1021 Allowance for Bad Debts	O		450.00		0.00		450.00	Net Current Liabilities	+7,020.00
1030 Merch. Inventory	O	925.00		0.00		925.00		**Operating cash flows**	**455.00**
1040 Prepaid Accounts	O	0.00		0.00		0.00			
								Investing Activities (I)	
1050 Fixed Assets	I	17,000.00		0.00		17,000.0 0		Net Fixed Assets	-17,000.00
1051 Accum. Depreciation	O		33.33		0.00		33.33	**Investing cash flows**	**-17,000.00**
LIABILITIES								**Financing Activities (F)**	
2010 Accounts Payable	O		700.00		0.00		700.00	Capital + LT Loan	+35,000.00
2020 Salaries & Wage Payable	O		320.00		0.00		320.00	**Financing cash flows**	**+35,000.0 0**
2030 Long-term Payable	F		15,000.00		0.00		15,000.0 0		
2040 Unearned Revenue	O		6,000.00		0.00		6,000.0 0	**Cash flows (O+I+F)**	**+18,455.0 0**
								Cash Jan. 1	**0.00**
EQUITY									

3010 Owner's Capital/Equity	F			20,000.00		0.00			20,000	Cash Bal. Jan. 31, 2017	+18,455.00
3020 Drawing	F										

The Statement of Cash Flows using the Indirect method:

Net Operating Cash Flows		
Net Income from Income Statement		2,876.67
Add Depreciation non-Cash expense		33.33
Change in Net Current Assets	-9,475.00	
Change in Net Current Liabilities	7,020.00	-2,455.00
		455.00
Net Investing Cash Flows		
Purchase of Office Furniture	-2000.00	
Purchase of Machinery	-15,000	**-17,000.00**
Net Financing Cash Flows		
Capital invested by owner	20,000.00	
Long Term Bank Loan	15,000.00	**35,000.00**
Total Change in Cash Position		**18,455.00**

Notes regarding the *indirect* cash flows method:

- The idea behind the indirect method is that, in accordance with the double-entry system of accounting, we can mathematically, indirectly determine the *changes* in the cash account by summing the changes in all the other (non-cash) accounts in the balance sheet for the period. *Changes* in the *cash* account represent opposite changes in the non-cash accounts: (a) *inflows* or receipt of cash from the *reduction* of the other assets and *increases* in liabilities; and (b) *outflows* or payment of cash to *increase* the non-cash asset amounts or *reduce* the balances in liability accounts.

    It might sound confusing at first, but if you think of the accounting equation, A = L + E, as *related to the cash account only* in simple arithmetic terms it might be easier to understand. Providing the liability and equity accounts in the balance sheet are held constant (unchanged), if the non-cash asset accounts were *reduced* (cash source), the *cash* account must be *increased* (cash used to increase cash balance) to keep the accounting equation in balance. It then follows, that an *increase* in the value of the *non-cash* asset accounts, would need a reduction in the *cash* account (cash source) for the accounting equation to remain in balance.

Similar reasoning using the accounting equation and simple arithmetic could also be applied to the (non-cash) liability accounts by holding the non-assets and equity accounts constant: if the amount in the *liabilities* accounts increased (increased debt as cash source), the *cash* account must also be increased (cash used to increase cash balance) to maintain the balance in the accounting equation.

A decrease in the value of the liabilities accounts would also need a in the cash account, all other non-cash and equity accounts remaining unchanged (constant). By combining the changes to the non-cash assets and liabilities accounts we can calculate the overall change in the cash account. This is what was meant earlier by "as related to the cash account only."

- The statement begins with the operating cash flows section starting with the net income (NI) or loss for the period under review.

- The net income (NI) amount includes non-cash expenses such as depreciation. This amount must be added back to the NI because they have no effect on *cash* for the period.

- Note that the amount for bad debt is also added back to NI only if the change to the accounts receivable (gross, not net receivable) is used in the calculation of total changes in the current assets; otherwise, using the changes in both accounts receivable and the allowance for bad debts for the period has the same effect as adding the bad debt expense for the period back to the NI.

- Depreciation expense is added back to NI because it is a non-cash item for the period.

The Bank Reconciliation Statement

The bank reconciliation is a tool used to provide detailed information about how much cash resources are legally owned by the organization on a specific date. Let me repeat this statement because it is extremely important for learners to grasp:

> The bank reconciliation statement is used to provide detailed information about how much cash resources on hand or in the bank is legally owned by the organization on a specific date.

The major question the reconciliation answers is: how much money does the business still legally own at the end of the month if all checks issued and bank service fees were paid, and the bank had recorded all deposits in the business' account, including any interest earned? When an individual or company opens an account with a financial institution, such as a bank or credit union, the individual or company receives a check book, deposit slips, and a *check register* to be used to keep track of the checks paid out and deposits made on a day to day basis.

A typical check register looks like the following table with a few minor changes: the author switched the *ADDITIONS* and *SUBTRACTIONS* sections and inserted reference letters (a) to (g) to make it easier for beginners to understand how the register is used.

PLEASE MAKE SURE TO DEDUCT CHARGES THAT AFFECT YOUR ACCOUNT							
ITEM NO. OR TRANS. CODE (a)	DATE (b)	TRANSACTION DESCRIPTION (c)	ADDITIONS: AMT OF DEPOSITS OR INTEREST (+) (d)	✔ T	FEE IF ANY (-) (e)	SUBTRACTIONS: AMT OF PAYMENTS OR WITHDRAWALS (-) (f)	BALANCE (g)

A reconciliation of the balance in the cash general ledger account in the books of the firm with the amount shown on the monthly statement sent by the bank, or digitally downloaded from and online-bank account, is called a bank reconciliation, and details are shown on a document called a Bank Reconciliation Statement as at a certain date.

As an example, MZ LLC uses the local bank, Sharks & Loans LLC, for the firm's daily banking business to deposit funds and make check payments.

We will need three documents to prepare a bank reconciliation statement as at January 31, 2017 for MZ LLC: (1) Previous bank reconciliation statement (since this is the first one, none is available), (2) printout of the general ledger cash account for the period, and (3) the current bank statement.

Printout of the General Ledger Cash Account

				General Ledger				
Account Name: Cash					Account No.: 1010			
				Post JL here		Updated Balance		
Date 2017		Trans. Description	JL Ref.	Debit	Credit	Debit	Credit	
Jan.	1	General Journal	J1	20,000.00		20,000.00	
Jan.	1	General Journal	J1		2,000.00	18,000.00	
Jan.	1	General Journal	J1		1,500.00	16,500.00	
Jan.	2	General Journal	J1		600.00	15,900.00	
Jan.	4	General Journal	J1		2,000.00	13,900.00	
Jan.	5	General Journal	J1		200.00	13,700.00	
Jan.	6	General Journal	J1		800.00	12,900.00	
Jan.	11	General Journal	J2		175.00	12,725.00	
Jan.	13	General Journal	J2		800.00	11,925.00	
Jan.	16	General Journal	J2		225.00	11,700.00	
Jan.	18	General Journal	J2		85.00	11,615.00	
Jan.	23	General Journal	J2	3,000.00		14,615.00	
Jan.	27	General Journal	J2		1,600.00	13,015.00	
Jan.	30	General Journal	J2	6,000.00		19,015.00	
Jan.	30	General Journal	J2		560.00	18,455.00	

Copy of the Bank Statement from Sharks & Loans LLC for January 31, 2017

STATEMENT OF ACCOUNT	SHARKS & LOANS LLC YOUR CITY, YOUR STATE, ZIP 99998			STATEMENT NO. 00004567
ACCOUNT NO.	**MONTH**			
999100	January 21, 2017			

MZ LLC

20 Anywhere Ave. Florida Town.

Florida City, FL. 12345

PREV. BALANCE	TOTAL CHECK AMT.	TOTAL DEPOSIT AMT.	BANK FEES	CLOSING BALANCE
0.00	8,300.00	23,000.00	0.00	14,700.00
MIN. BALANCE	**NUMBER OF CHECKS**	**NUMBER OF DEPOSITS**	**AVERAGE BAL.**	
11,700.00	9	2	14,765.63	

CHECKING ACCOUNT ACTIVITIES RECORDED FOR THE MONTH

DATE	CHECK AMOUNTS	CHECK AMOUNTS	DEPOSITS	BALANCE
January 1			20,000.00	20,000.00
January 3	2,000.00	1,500.00		16,500.00
January 5	600.00			15,900.00
January 8	200.00	2,000.00		13,700.00
January 10	800.00			12,900.00
January 14	175.00			12,725.00
January 19	800.00	225.00		11,700.00
January 24			3,000.00	14,700.00
		January 31, 2017 Ending Balance		14,700.00

Using the printout of the cash account from the general ledger and the bank statement, all transactions for the month are compared and transactions appearing in both documents are crossed out. Transactions not crossed out on the printout of the general ledger cash account are then used to adjust the ending balance amount on the bank statement in the reconciliation statement: outstanding deposits (called deposit in transit) are added and check outstanding are deducted from the *bank statement balance*. The results would look like the following:

Printout of general ledger and bank statement showing the amounts deposited and checks paid for the period which appeared in both statements crossed out.

General Ledger							
Account Name: Cash				Account No.: 1010			
				Post JL here		Updated Balance	
Date 2017		Trans. Description	JL Ref.	Debit	Credit	Debit	Credit
Jan.	1	General Journal	J1	20,000.00		20,000.00	
Jan.	1	General Journal	J1		2,000.00	18,000.00	
Jan.	1	General Journal	J1		1,500.00	16,500.00	
Jan.	2	General Journal	J1		600.00	15,900.00	
Jan.	4	General Journal	J1		2,000.00	13,900.00	
Jan.	5	General Journal	J1		200.00	13,700.00	
Jan.	6	General Journal	J1		800.00	12,900.00	
Jan.	11	General Journal	J2		175.00	12,725.00	
Jan.	13	General Journal	J2		800.00	11,925.00	
Jan.	16	General Journal	J2		225.00	11,700.00	
Jan.	18	General Journal	J2		85.00	11,615.00	
Jan.	23	General Journal	J2	3,000.00		14,615.00	
Jan.	27	General Journal	J2		1,600.00	13,015.00	
Jan.	30	General Journal	J2	6,000.00		19,015.00	
Jan.	30	General Journal	J2		560.00	18,455.00	

STATEMENT OF ACCOUNT	SHARKS & LOANS LLC YOUR CITY, YOUR STATE, ZIP 99998			STATEMENT NO. 00004567
ACCOUNT NO.	MONTH			
999100	January 21, 2017			

	MZ LLC 20 Anywhere Ave. Florida Town. Florida City, FL. 12345			
PREV. BALANCE	TOTAL CHECK AMT.	TOTAL DEPOSIT AMT.	BANK FEES	CLOSING BALANCE
0.00	8,300.00	23,000.00	0.00	14,700.00
MIN. BALANCE	NUMBER OF CHECKS	NUMBER OF DEPOSITS	AVERAGE BAL.	
11,700.00	9	2	14,765.63	

CHECKING ACCOUNT ACTIVITIES RECORDED FOR THE MONTH

DATE	CHECK AMOUNTS	CHECK AMOUNTS	DEPOSITS	BALANCE
January 1			20,000.00	20,000.00
January 3	2,000.00	1,500.00		16,500.00
January 5	600.00			15,900.00
January 8	200.00	2,000.00		13,700.00
January 10	800.00			12,900.00
January 14	175.00			12,725.00
January 19	800.00	225.00		11,700.00
January 24			3,000.00	14,700.00
		January 31, 2017 Ending Balance		14,700.00

The bank reconciliation statement for January 31, 2017, showing the adjusted balances in the general ledger and the adjusted bank statement amount showing deposits in transit and outstanding check not yet recorded at the bank, would appear as follows:

Bank Reconciliation of MZ LLC for Month Ending January 31, 2017	C/O	General Ledger	Bank Statement
Balances as at January 31, 2017		$18,455.00	$14,700.00
Add Deposits in Transit:			
Jan. 30 $6,000.00	O		+ $6,000.00
Less Checks Outstanding:			
Jan. 18 check #010 $85.00	O		
Jan. 27 check #011 $1,600.00	O		
Jan. 30 check #012 $560.00	O		-2,245.00
Less bank service charges not posted to GL to be JL			
Reconciled Balances showing actual cash owned		$18,455.00	$18,455.00

Notes: C/O = items cleared or outstanding—not yet presented or posted at the bank. The strikethrough of the amounts signifies that the amounts have been presented and posted to both systems.

Summary

We have now completed coverage of the main financial statements: Income Statement, Changes in Owner's Equity, and Balance Sheet in chapter 7; and the Cash Flows Statement in this chapter. The cash flows statement can be presented in two formats: direct, and indirect. The statement of cash flows provides a summary of the sources and uses of cash for a business, categorized as operating, financing, and investing. The reason and mechanics of completing bank reconciliation for an organization was also discussed in this chapter. The bank reconciliation is used to determine the amount of cash legally available to be used by the firm at the end of the period.

Chapter 9: Basic Introduction to Financial Ratios and Trend Analysis

Question: What is the purpose of this chapter?

Answer: Introduction to popular accounting tools used to analyze the results of a firm's operating systems and managerial results compared to competitors and industry metrics.

This book is written for new learners of accounting and bookkeeping therefore only a brief introduction and description of financial ratios and trend analysis will be presented. Detailed analyses and explanations can be found in more advanced accounting books. Financial ratios and trend analyses are tools used by accountants in analyzing and reporting on the performance of the organization over time and compared with ratios of competitors and the industry in which the organization operates. The ratios and trend analyses are calculated from data shown on comparative balance sheets and income statements of the firm and its competitors.

The information derived from the ratios and trend analyses are used by individuals within and outside of the firm, and other organizations, for various decision-making purposes. Information provided by financial analyses are usually grouped into three main areas: (1) profitability (how profitable is the business?), (2) solvency (will the firm be able to continue in the foreseeable future?), and (3) liquidity (will the firm be able to pay its debts when due?). Individuals such as, managers, employees, creditors, loan officers of banks, the government, and owners and investors are collectively referred to in accounting as *stakeholders*. The following is an overview of vertical and horizontal analysis of few of the more common ratios used for comparison, decision-making, and strategic purposes used for decision making.

Trend Analysis

Trend analyses look at changes in the amounts (balances) of the elements or general ledger accounts in the income statement and balance sheet over time to assess the possible effects on the operating performance and profitability of the organization. Two types of trend analyses are (1) Vertical analysis and (2) Horizontal analysis.

Vertical Analysis

Trend comparisons using the balance sheet and income statement are usually done by first converting them to percentages: the elements (accounts) of the *balance sheet* are converted to percentages based on total assets for each period, with *total assets* representing 100 percent; whereas the accounts (elements) of the *income statement* are converted to percentages of *net sales*, with net sales representing 100 percent for the period. This conversion of balance sheet and income statement accounts to percentages for comparison purposes is referred to as converting them to *similar sizes* of 100 percent. By using similar-sized comparative balance sheets and income statements trends can be identified and comparisons can be made between organizations of different types and sizes, or between organizations in different industries.

Converting the Income Statement and Balance Sheet to similar-sized statements entail adding columns to show the percentages next to the related amounts as shown below. The following amounts were created and used for illustration purposes only.

COMPARATIVE BALANCE SHEET

Comparative Balance Sheet as at December 31, 2017

			Dec. 31, 2017	Dec. 31, 2016	
Assets	%	$$	$$	%	$$
Cash	19.76		7,000.00	18.86	6275.00
Accounts Receivable	16.94	6,000.00			
Less Allowance for Bad Debts	-0.64	-225.00			
Net Accounts Receivable	16.30		5,775.00	15.03	5000.00
Merchandise Inventory	16.94		6000.00	21.04	7000.00
Total Current Assets	53.00		18,775.00	54.92	18,275.00
Fixed Assets	47.99	17,000.00			
Less Accumulated Depreciation	-0.99	-350.00			
Net Fixed Assets	47.00		16,650.00		15000.00
Total Assets (A)	100.00		**$35,425.00**	100.00	**$33,275.00**
Liabilities					
Accounts Payable	7.76		2750.00	10.22	3401.00
Salaries & Wages Payable	2.48		880.00	1.95	650.00
Unearned Revenue	7.06		2,500.00	4.51	1500.00
Total Current Liabilities	17.30		6,130.00	16.68	5,551.00
Long-term Payable	33.87		12,000.00	36.06	12000.00
Total Liabilities (L)	51.18		**$18,130.00**	52.75	**$17,551.00**
Owners' Equity					
Owners' Capital/Equity	28.23		10,000.00	30.05	10000.00
Retained Earnings	20.59		7,295.00	17.20	5724.00
Total Equity (E)	48.82		**$17,295.00**	47.25	**$15,724.00**
Total Liabilities + Equity (L+E) = (A)	100.00		**$35,425.00**	100.00	**$33,275.00**

COMPARATIVE INCOME STATEMENT

Comparative Income Statement
For Period Ended December 31, 2017

	2017		2016	
Sales Revenue	%	$	%	$
Sales:	100.00	18,000.00	100.00	14,000.00
Less Cost of Goods Sold:	33.33	6,000.00	33.33	4,666.20
Gross Profit	66.67	12,000.00	66.67	9,333.80
Expenses	%	$	%	$
Rent Expense	9.44	1,700.00	10.71	1,500.00
Salaries & Wages	19.44	3,500.00	21.43	3,000.00
Office Expenses & Supplies	1.25	225.00	1.07	150.00
Utilities Expense	3.06	550.00	2.32	325.00
Insurance Expense	6.67	1,200.00	7.14	1,000.00
Advertising & Promotion Expense	5.00	900.00	5.36	750.00
Depreciation Expense	3.61	650.00	2.50	350.00
Vehicle, Trav. & Ent. Expenses	5.44	980.00	5.50	770.00
Bad Debt Expenses	4.03	725.00	3.75	525.00
Total Expenses	57.94	10,430.00	59.79	8,370.00
Net Income/(Loss)	8.73	1,570.00	6.88	963.80

Horizontal Analysis

Horizontal analysis looks at changes in the elements of the financial statements over time and usually between two consecutive operating periods. The first step in horizontal analysis is the construction of two additional columns in the comparative financial statements, one to show the dollar change of each major element in the statement, and the other to calculate the percentage of the change based on the previous period amount. First, we subtract the amount in the previous period from the equivalent in the most current period. For example, in the illustrations that follow, the amounts in the 2016 column are subtracted from the amounts in the 2017 column to create the amounts in the column titled $ Change. Next, we divide the $ Change amounts by the 2016 $ amounts and convert them to percentages, to populate the percentages in the % Change column.

The following tables and amounts are used for our demonstration of horizontal analysis of financial statements and created for illustration purposes only.

Chapter 9: Basic Introduction to Financial Ratios and Trend Analysis

COMPARATIVE BALANCE SHEET

Comparative Balance Sheet as at December 31, 2017

	% Change	$ Change	Dec. 2017 $$	Dec. 2016 $$
Assets				
Cash	11.55	725.00	7,000.00	6275.00
Accounts Receivable				
Less Allowance for Bad Debts				
Net Accounts Receivable	15.50	775.00	5,775.00	5000.00
Merchandise Inventory	-14.29	-1,000.00	6000.00	7000.00
Total Current Assets	2.74	500.00	18,775.00	18,275.00
Fixed Assets				
Less Accumulated Depreciation				
Net Fixed Assets	11.00	1,650.00	16,650.00	15000.00
Total Assets (A)	**6.46**	2,150.00	$35,425.00	$33,275.00
Liabilities				
Accounts Payable	-19.14	-651.00	2750.00	3401.00
Salaries & Wages Payable	35.38	230.00	880.00	650.00
Unearned Revenue	66.67	1,000.00	2,500.00	1500.00
Total Current Liabilities	10.43	579.00	6,130.00	5,551.00
Long-term Payable	0.00	0.00	12,000.00	12000.00
Total Liabilities (L)	3.30	579.00	$18,130.00	$17,551.00
Owners' Equity				
Owners' Capital/Equity	0.00	0.00	10,000.00	10000.00
Retained Earnings	27.45	1,571.00	7,295.00	5724.00
Total Equity (E)	9.99	1,571.00	$17,295.00	$15,724.00
Total Liabilities + Equity (L+E) = (A)	**6.46**	2,150.00	$35,425.00	$33,275.00

Summary of steps taken to create the data to be used for horizontal analysis of financial statements:

1. Insert two additional columns to the left of the 2017 amounts in the financial statements to be used for (a) change in the dollar amounts for each element of the statement between 2016 and 2017 ($ Change column), and (b) conversion of the changes to percentages (% Change column);

2. Deduct the amounts in the 2016 column from the amounts in the 2017 column to fill the $ Change column;

3. Divide the amounts in the $ Change column by the amounts in the 2016 column and convert the ratio to percentages to fill the % column.

COMPARATIVE INCOME STATEMENT

Comparative Income Statement
For Period Ended December 31, 2017

	% Change	$ Change	2017 $	2016 $
Sales Revenue				
Sales:	28.57	4,000.00	18,000.00	14,000.00
Less Cost of Goods Sold:	28.57	1,333.80	6,000.00	4,666.20
Gross Profit	**28.57**	**2,666.20**	**12,000.00**	**9,333.80**
Expenses			$	$
Rent Expense	13.33	200.00	1,700.00	1,500.00
Salaries & Wages	16.67	500.00	3,500.00	3,000.00
Office Expenses & Supplies	50.00	75.00	225.00	150.00
Utilities Expense	69.23	225.00	550.00	325.00
Insurance Expense	20.00	200.00	1,200.00	1,000.00
Advertising & Promotion Expense	20.00	150.00	900.00	750.00
Depreciation Expense	85.71	300.00	650.00	350.00
Vehicle, Trav. & Ent. Expenses	27.27	210.00	980.00	770.00
Bad Debt Expenses	38.10	200.00	725.00	525.00
Total Expenses	**24.61**	**2,060.00**	**10,430.00**	**8,370.00**
Net Income/(Loss)	**62.90**	**606.20**	**1,570.00**	**963.80**

Financial Ratios

Examples of some common ratios for 2017 are shown below and identified as profitability (P), liquidity (L), and solvency (S), and the financial statements associated with their calculations.

- Working capital (L) is the difference between current assets and current liabilities as shown on the balance sheet. Source balance sheet. 18,775 – 6,130 = 12,645

- Current ratio (L) is current assets divided by current liabilities. Source balance sheet. 18,775 / 6,130 = 3.06

- Quick ratio (L) is the current assets minus the merchandise inventory, divided by current liabilities. Source balance sheet (18,775 – 6,000) / 6,130 = 2.08

- Gross Profit margin (P) is net sales minus cost of goods sold (COGS) to provide a gross profit amount which is then divided by the net sales. This is also called contribution margin. Source income statement (12,000 / 18,000) x 100 = 66.67%

- Net Income ratio (P) to net sales is net income divided by net sales. Source Income Statement (1,570 /18,000) x 100 = 8.73%

Chapter 9: Basic Introduction to Financial Ratios and Trend Analysis

- Return on assets (P) is net income divided by average total assets for the period. Sources income statement and balance sheet 1,570 / ((35,425 + 33,275)/2) x 100 = (1,570 / 34,350) x 100 = 4.57%

- Asset turnover (L) is net sales divided by the average total assets for the period. Sources income statement and balance sheet 18,000 / ((35,425 + 33,275)/2) = (18,000 / 34,350 = 0.52

- Accounts receivable turnover (L) is net sales on terms (credit) divided by the average net accounts receivable for the period. Sources income statement and balance sheet 18,000 / ((5,775 + 5000)/2) = 18,000 / 5,387.50 = 3.34

- Merchandise inventory turnover (L) ratio is cost of goods sold divided by the average merchandise inventory for the period. income statement and balance sheet 6,000 / ((6,000 + 7,000)/2) = 6,000 / 6,500 = 0.92

- Debt to Assets ratio (S) is total liabilities divided by total Assets (notice the accounting equation). Source balance sheet 18,130 / 35,425 = 0.51

- Debt to Equity ratio (S) is total liabilities divided by total owner's equity (notice the accounting equation). Source balance sheet 18,130 / 17,295 = 1.05

Notice that some of the ratios are converted to percentages.

Summary

Financial analyses are activities done by experienced accountants and financial analysts to provide information useful for decision-making by users of financial statements. The basic concepts related to trend analyses, including vertical and horizontal analyses, and financial ratios were introduced in this chapter. Learners interested in learning more about these concepts and interpretations are encouraged to seek more advanced books on accounting and finance.

Chapter 10: Final Thoughts and Encouragement

Steps in The Accounting Process					
__STEP 1__	__STEP 2__	__STEP 3__	__STEP 4__	__STEP 5__	__STEP 6__
Analyze Transactions	Record Journal Entries	Post to General Ledger	Prepare Trial Balance	End-of Period Adj. Entries	Compile Financial Reports

Before providing final thoughts on where we have been in the previous nine chapters, I wish to express my appreciation and thanks for taking this journey with me. I hope you learned a great deal from this trip.

General journals were used in the examples in the book because many computerized accounting software systems available for business use require a good understanding of how to journalize transactions, although some transaction entries in computerized accounting systems are created by the recording and posting of documents such as invoices and checks. This is important to know because once transactions are recorded and saved in a computerized accounting system, the other steps, except for the adjustments, in the accounting process can be automatically generated by the program.

In chapter 1 we learned that accounting is both a process and a means of summarizing and reporting of financial transactions and activities of a business for specific periods; that accounting is a systematic step-by-step set of activities taken by the accountant to (1) identify, analyze and record financial transactions, (2) record the transactions in the journal using a chart of accounts, (3) post the journal entries to the general ledger, (4) prepare a trial balance of the general ledger accounts, (5) make adjustments at the end of accounting periods, and (6) summarize and report on the activities of the firm.

Each chapter was dedicated to introducing and demonstrating concepts and activities involved in each of the systematic steps in the accounting process:

1. In chapter 1 we introduced the two most important concepts to learn in accounting, (1) the accounting equation and (2) the double-entry concept of accounting, upon which all modern accounting systems are based.

2. In chapter 2 we defined business transactions and introduced the chart of accounts (COA) and the general journal (GJ) and demonstrated how they are used to record the business transactions of an organization.

3. The general ledger (GL) and trial balance (TB) were discussed in chapter 3, along

with the concept of "T" accounts.

4. In chapter 4 we discussed the general accounts—elements that make up the balance sheet of the firm, and defined the major classification found in the balance sheet: assets, liabilities, and equity. These provide details of the relationships found in the accounting equation. The difference between an expense and expenditure was also explained in the chapter.

5. We described the elements—general ledger accounts found in the income statement along with the two main classifications, revenue and expenses, in chapter 5.

6. In chapter 6 we looked at steps 4 and 5 involving end-of-period activities including adjusting entries, closing entries, and the income summary account and briefly introduced the concept of net income.

7. Chapters 7 and 8 were devoted to step 6, financial reporting statements: the income statement, the balance sheet, changes in owner's equity, and the cash flows statement. We also explored the direct and indirect methods of preparing cash flows statements along with the bank reconciliation statement in chapter 8.

8. A brief introduction of financial ratios and trend analysis was provided in chapter 9. Details of these concepts were not provided as financial ratios and trend analyses are generally done by more advanced and experienced accountants.

You have now been formally introduced to what bookkeeping and accounting is about and can see that the subject can be learned with minimum knowledge of mathematics. I encourage you to visit a public library or your favorite online bookstore to further explore the self-help, introductory, or other accounting resources that are available.

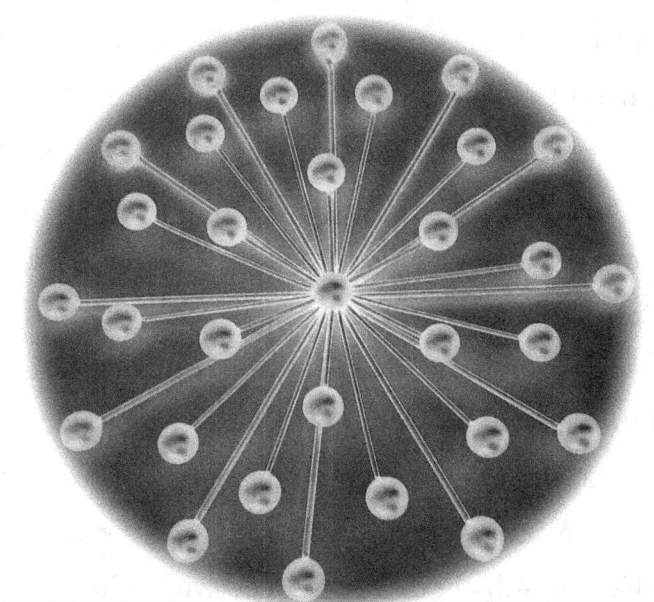

Collaborative learning. "Superior learners seek at least two to six additional sources of information." Dr. Denver Pettigrew

Appendixes

Appendix A: Combined Chart of Accounts and Trial Balance

<table>
<tr><td colspan="3" align="center">A simple Combined Chart of Accounts and Trial Balance</td></tr>
<tr><td align="center">CHART OF ACCOUNTS</td><td colspan="2" align="center">TRIAL BALANCE</td></tr>
<tr><td>Account #, Classification and General Ledger</td><td>Debit $$</td><td><b>Credit $$</td></tr>
<tr><td>Descriptions</td><td></td><td></td></tr>
<tr><td>Balance Sheet</td><td></td><td></td></tr>
<tr><td>Assets: 1000</td><td></td><td></td></tr>
<tr><td>• 1010 Cash</td><td>XXXX.XX</td><td></td></tr>
<tr><td>• 1020 Accounts Receivable</td><td>XXXX.XX</td><td></td></tr>
<tr><td>• 1021 Allowance for Bad Debts</td><td></td><td>XXXX.XX</td></tr>
<tr><td>• 1030 Merchandise Inventory</td><td>XXXX.XX</td><td></td></tr>
<tr><td>• 1040 Prepaid Accounts</td><td>XXXX.XX</td><td></td></tr>
<tr><td>• 1050 Fixed Assets</td><td>XXXX.XX</td><td></td></tr>
<tr><td>• 1051 Accumulated Depreciation</td><td></td><td>XXXX.XX</td></tr>
<tr><td>Liabilities: 2000</td><td></td><td></td></tr>
<tr><td>• 2010 Accounts Payable</td><td></td><td>XXXX.XX</td></tr>
<tr><td>• 2020 Salaries & Wages Payable</td><td></td><td>XXXX.XX</td></tr>
<tr><td>• 2030 Long-term Payable</td><td></td><td>XXXX.XX</td></tr>
<tr><td>• 2040 Unearned Revenue</td><td></td><td>XXXX.XX</td></tr>
<tr><td>Equity: 3000</td><td></td><td></td></tr>
<tr><td>• 3010 Owner's Capital/Equity</td><td></td><td>XXXX.XX</td></tr>
<tr><td>• 3020 Drawing</td><td>XXXX.XX</td><td></td></tr>
<tr><td>• 3030 Retained Earnings</td><td></td><td>XXXX.XX</td></tr>
<tr><td>Income Statement</td><td></td><td></td></tr>
<tr><td>Revenue: 4000</td><td></td><td></td></tr>
<tr><td>• 4010 Sales Revenue</td><td></td><td>XXXX.XX</td></tr>
<tr><td>• 4020 Other Revenue</td><td></td><td>XXXX.XX</td></tr>
<tr><td>• 4030 Cost of Goods Sold (COGS)</td><td>XXXX.XX</td><td></td></tr>
<tr><td>Expenses: 5000</td><td></td><td></td></tr>
<tr><td>• 5010 Rent Expense</td><td>XXXX.XX</td><td></td></tr>
<tr><td>• 5020 Salaries & Wages</td><td>XXXX.XX</td><td></td></tr>
<tr><td>• 5030 Office Expenses & Supplies</td><td>XXXX.XX</td><td></td></tr>
<tr><td>• 5040 Telephone Expense</td><td>XXXX.XX</td><td></td></tr>
<tr><td>• 5050 Insurance Expense</td><td>XXXX.XX</td><td></td></tr>
<tr><td>• 5060 Advertising & Promotion Expense</td><td>XXXX.XX</td><td></td></tr>
<tr><td>• 5070 Depreciation Expense</td><td>XXXX.XX</td><td></td></tr>
<tr><td>• 5080 Vehicle, Travelling & Entertainment Expense</td><td>XXXX.XX</td><td></td></tr>
<tr><td>• 5090 Bad Debt Expense</td><td>XXXX.XX</td><td></td></tr>
<tr><td></td><td>XXXX.XX</td><td>XXXX.XX</td></tr>
</table>

(Right margin labels: BALANCE SHEET, INCOME STATEMENT)

Appendix B: General Journal

Date 20___		Description	GL Ref.	Debit	Credit
		General Journal			Page No._____

Appendix C: General Ledger

General Ledger							
Account Name:						Account No.:_____	
Date 20__		Trans. Description	JL Ref.	Post JL here		Updated Balance	
				Debit	Credit	Debit	Credit

Appendix D: Combined Income Statement & Retained Earnings

Combined Income Statement & Retained Earnings For Period Ended _____ , 20____		
Sales Revenue	$	$
Sales:		
Less Cost of Goods Sold:		
Gross Profit		
Expenses	$	$
Rent Expense		
Salaries & Wages		
Office Expenses & Supplies		
Telephone Expense		
Insurance Expense		
Advertising & Promotion Expense		
Depreciation Expense		
Vehicle, Trav. & Ent. Expenses		
Bad Debt Expenses		
Total Expenses		
Net Income		
Add Previous Retained Earnings Balance		
Less Drawings by Owner for Period		
Current Y/E Retained Earnings Balance		

Appendixes

Appendix E: Balance Sheet

Balance Sheet as at Period Ending _____ , 20 ____	$$	$$
Assets		
Cash		
Accounts Receivable		
Less Allowance for Bad Debts		
Net Accounts Receivable		
Merchandise Inventory		
Current Assets		
Fixed Assets		
Less Accumulated Depreciation		
Net Fixed Assets		
Total Assets (A)		
Liabilities		
Accounts Payable		
Salaries & Wages Payable		
Current Liabilities		
Long-term Payable		
Unearned Revenue		
Long-term Liabilities		
Total Liabilities (L)		
Owners' Equity		
Owners' Capital/Equity		
Drawing		
Retained Earnings		
Total Equity (E)		
Total Liabilities + Equity (L+E) = (A)		

Appendix F: Typical Check Register

PLEASE MAKE SURE TO DEDUCT CHARGES THAT AFFECT YOUR ACCOUNT								
ITEM NO. OR TRANS. CODE (a)	DATE (b)	TRANSACTION DESCRIPTION (c)	ADDITIONS: AMT OF DEPOSITS OR INTEREST (+) (d)		✔ T	FEE IF ANY (-) (e)	SUBTRACTIONS: AMT OF PAYMENTS OR WITHDRAWALS (-) (f)	BALANCE (g)